Great Wilderness Days

in the words of JOHN BURROUGHS

A final gleam of sunlight over Tupper Lake in the Adirondacks marks the peaceful end of day.

"The seasons came and went, each with its own charms and enticements. I was ready for each and contented with each."

At a colorful pond such as this, Burroughs could witness the "moist, spongy, tranquil, luxurious side of Nature."

Great Wilderness Days

in the words of JOHN BURROUGHS

By the Editors of
Country Beautiful

Country Beautiful
Waukesha, Wisconsin

Opposite: *Spring marks the return of the birds. A mourning dove quietly sits in her nest among the lush, green foliage of spring.*

COUNTRY BEAUTIFUL: *Publisher and Editorial Director:* Michael P. Dineen; *Vice President, Editorial:* Robert L. Polley; *Vice President, Operations:* Donna Griesemer; *House Editor:* John M. Nuhn; *Contributing Editor:* Beth McKenty; *Senior Editors:* Kenneth L. Schmitz, James H. Robb, Stewart L. Udall; *Art Director:* Buford Nixon; *Associate Editors:* Kay Kundinger, Jeanie Holzwart.

Country Beautiful Corporation is a wholly owned subsidiary of Flick-Reedy Corporation: President: Frank Flick.

PHOTO CREDITS: Thomas Algire, 161; American Museum of Natural History from the John Burroughs Memorial Society, 188 through 208; Ron Austing from Photo Researchers, 55; William A. Bake, 32-33; Betty Bellinger, 181; British Tourist Authority, 128, 129; Bureau of Sport Fisheries and Wildlife, 170; Robert Carr, 4, 13, 44, 61, 93, 149, 151; Ed Cooper, 1, 48, 111, 112-113, 120, 122, 143, 148, 172; Ted Czolowski, 116-117; H.L. Daggett, 70-71; Jerome Drown, 82; Michael Ederegger, 158; Michael and Christine Fong, 168; Leonard E. Foote, 30, 57; Freelance Photographers Guild by Jack Breed, 155; French Cultural Services, 131; Albert Gates, 2-3, 43, 89; Charles P. George, 88; Olive Glasgow, 79, 96, 167; Gottscho-Schleisner, 81; Josepha Haveman, 39, 41, 86-87, 138, 160; Robert Holland, 22-23; Ed Hutchins, 19; James P. Jackson, 51; Jamaica Tourist Board, 132-133; Ray Janusiak, 125; G.C. Kelley, 47, 54, 62, 65, 67, 119, 171; Jerry Kiesow, 31; Carl Kurtz, 76-77; Gary Ladd, 146-147; Thomas Peters Lake, 102-103, 156-157, 178-179; Wilford L. Miller, 53; Milwaukee Public Museum, 142; Thomas F. Monser, 75; David Muench, 108-109, 123; National Park Service, 126, 134; Hank Nielsen, 98; Charles P. Noyes, 177; John M. Nuhn, 42, 145, 164; Robert Nuhn, 100-101; Gary Randorf, 182-183; Robert Reynolds, 115; Charles M. Sheridan, 28; Clyde H. Smith, 16-17, 72; Dick Smith, 20, 24, 91, 105, 187; Dan Sudia, 68, 84; John Tveten, 34, 56, 58, 59, 64, 69; Upitis Color Studios, 10-11, 27, 107, 185; U.S. Forest Service, 94; Glenn Van Nimwegen, 8-9, 40; Brad Vogel, 14; Kenneth A. Wilson, 35, 46; Carl Wohl, 140-141; Gus Wolfe, 153; Jerome Wyckoff, 36, 136-137, 144, 162; Barbara Young, 159, 175.

Selections from John Burroughs's *The Summit of the Years,* copyright 1913, renewed 1941;. *The Breath of Life,* copyright 1915, renewed 1940; *Leaf and Tendril,* copyright 1908, renewed 1935; *Camping and Tramping with Roosevelt,* copyright 1907, renewed 1935; *Under the Apple Trees,* copyright 1916, renewed 1944; *Time and Change,* copyright 1912, renewed 1940; all copyrights renewed by Julian Burroughs; all selections reprinted by permission of Houghton Mifflin Company. Quote on page 8 from *John Burroughs —Boy and Man,* edited by Dr. Clara Barrus, copyright 1920 by Doubleday & Company, Inc. Text on pages 207-208 copyright *The Conservationist,* Albany, N.Y.

Contents

Preface 12

I Boyhood and Youth:
The Quality of Gratitude 14

II In the Shadow of the Catskills . . . 26

III John-of-the-Birds 54

IV Great Wilderness Days 80

V In the Western Wilderness 108

VI On Nature Abroad 126

VII Camping in the Wilderness 136

VIII The Inner Vision 150

IX An Open Door to God 172

Portrait of a Naturalist 186

Remembering John Burroughs . . 206

Appendix: Winners of
Burroughs Medal 208

"The most precious things in life are near at hand, without money and without price. Each of you has the whole wealth of the universe at your very door. All that I ever had, or still have, may be yours by stretching forth your hand and taking it."

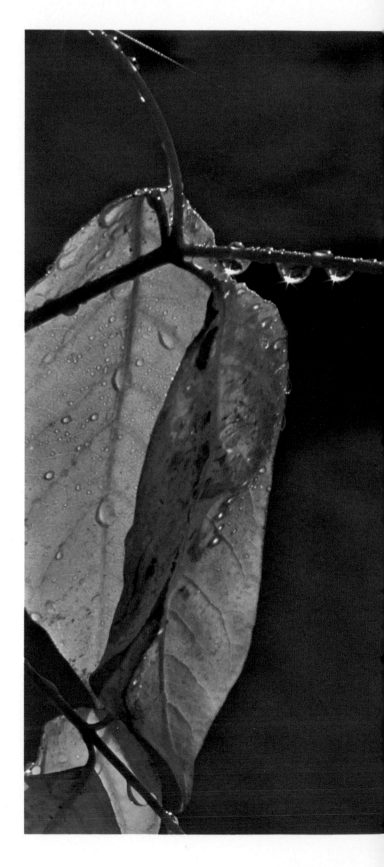

Early morning is a time for discovering the delicacies of nature. Raindrops sparkling in the sunlight add to the beauty of a new day.

Overleaf: *Filled with floating ice, the Hudson River flows past snow-laden trees near Burroughs's beloved home, Riverby.*

"A fall of snow, and this icy uproar is instantly hushed, the river sleeps in peace."

Preface

Born in 1837, John Burroughs lived during a time when the North American continent was still relatively wild and undeveloped. Millions of buffalo roamed the Western plains and while the Eastern Seaboard had been settled and passes found to the West, there were vast reaches of unbroken forest between the Appalachians and the Rockies. This was the time of Westward Ho and the wagon trains, of Indians, mountain men, and *voyageurs*, a quarter of a century before the Civil War, a period of tremendous growth and movement colored by romantic illusions as to what this great unexplored wilderness really was like. James Fenimore Cooper set the tone with his "Leatherstocking Tales," with Emerson, Walt Whitman and Thoreau building a new philosophy in intellectual thought.

While the Catskills and Adirondacks of New York State were home to him, it was Riverby, his farm on the banks of the mighty Hudson River, Slabsides, his hidden retreat, and his bark study at Riverby where he really belonged. I once visited Riverby long after his passing in 1921 and went to his bark study, the little writing place sheathed in native chestnut bark. Though it had not been used for years, it had not changed; papers and books were on the table, his wastebasket full of discarded notes. I felt as I stood there that he must have just stepped outside to listen to some bird or to smell the sweet spring air with its fragrance of bursting buds and warming earth.

He traveled widely in Europe but England must have meant most to him for here were the poets and writers he knew and cherished. He saw the blue Caribbean and Hawaii with its sandy beaches and palm-fringed shores, the Rockies and the Sierras, the coastal forests with their big trees, the glaciers and mountains of Alaska. He met John Muir in Yosemite, was a personal friend of President Theodore Roosevelt and many other eminent and devoted figures, but I always felt that while he treasured these relationships with famous men, he felt more at home with the woodchucks, thrushes and warblers of his native woods and those who came to visit him there. He loved people, especially children and all who knew joy in awareness and beauty.

He wrote for them of bird songs, the wind in the trees, and chuckling brooks, describing the changing seasons, the lushness of summer, the flaming colors of autumn, the starkness of winter snows, the awakening of life in the spring. He spoke of thunderstorms and lightning and howling gales with wonder and delight, wrote as he talked with the ease and naturalness that comes when one is in love with all nature.

His was a genuine love of living things and through his work he shows it in many different ways, that the soul and spirit and one's own living is what counted most and only when the real is seen with emotion and knowledge could one hope to find a niche in the hearts of others. He felt intuitively that this was what true literature treasured and that an artist, no matter what his field, must give of himself. There is no doubt that here was the secret of being able to share his life with many and the devotion and love of countless thousands proved he was right.

Ice forms interesting patterns around pebbles. Burroughs saw wonderment in the smallest natural phenomenon.

His writing shows amazement at the smallest natural phenomenon. Watching the first flowers pushing up through the sodden brown leaves after a long New England winter, or finding the nest of a rare warbler after much waiting and searching were exciting triumphs to him and readers could not help but share the thrills that were his. At the same time, there was an earthiness about him and a feeling of identity with the land itself. He was as indigenous as the lichen-covered boulders in his stone walls.

John Burroughs was a great interpretive naturalist who, day by day and month by month, lived constantly out of doors, pursuing his patient, painstaking observations and studies in an all-absorbing devotion toward the ultimate goal of capturing what he saw and felt in his books.

Great Wilderness Days in the Words of John Burroughs has caught the real meaning of his work inasmuch as wilderness to him was the epitome of what was natural. It meant the woods and fields around his home, the Catskills and the Adirondacks, and the many places he had visited. Wilderness did not necessarily mean unbroken reaches of wild country but could be found in a thicket of honeysuckle, a patch of tundra above timberline, or a little swamp fed by a spring.

As he approached the end of his roaming, he dwelt more and more on the deeper and hidden meanings of wilderness. Never bored or feeling that the secrets of nature were becoming commonplace, he was filled with awe and wonderment over what he had seen and known. He believed in a Primal Will revealed through order and beauty and once wrote, "Each of you has the whole wealth of the universe at your very door," a concept few knew as well as he. Through these gleanings from a lifetime of writing runs a golden thread, the thought that the key to fulfillment is being in tune with the cosmos and ancient rhythms and at one with every living thing.

—Sigurd F. Olson

Summer 1974

Boyhood and Youth:
The Quality of Gratitude

John Burroughs's life was a journey in search of his own place. In childhood, he experienced the peculiar rejection given to the child who is not quite the same as the others in a family. He could recall visitors looking over his brothers and sisters, then pointing to him and saying to his parents, "But this one, this is not your boy —who is he?"

In a family where learning was practical instruction in plowing land and making butter, he yearned for books and for facts about nature. It was not enough that crops were planted and harvested, or that orchards yielded fruit. He wanted to know about growth and fruition, about the purposes underlying the crops, about the universe as revealed in his tiny corner of it.

He was a naturalist steeped in rural ways, having been brought up near Roxbury, New York, and although his horizons were broadened by travel and association with eminent persons, he was secure in the limited domain chosen as his own.

The one time he asked his father for help with school expenses, he was refused. To the older brother, Hiram, who answered that appeal, he later provided assistance and shelter for many years, but it satisfied him greatly that he was also able, through the proceeds of his nature writing, to assist his father and mother and make their declining years free of want. In fact, most of his brothers and sisters benefited from his literary earnings, although none of them read his books or were familiar with his work.

At the end of his life, composing his memoirs at the request of his son, Julian, Burroughs wrote:

I have spoken of my good luck. It began in my being born on a farm, of parents in the prime of their days, and in humble circumstances. I deem it good luck too that my birth fell in April, a month in which so many other things find it good to begin life.

Gratitude, that rare quality, many times shines through his writings. The land, mountains, streams, birds, animals, immense areas of virgin forest and the sky overhead fed the inner light of Burroughs, helping the careful spectator and reporter of nature to emerge from the introverted child.

Opposite: "In youth I saw nature as a standing invitation to come forth and give play to myself; . . . the woods were for hunting and exploring, and for all kinds of sylvan adventure."

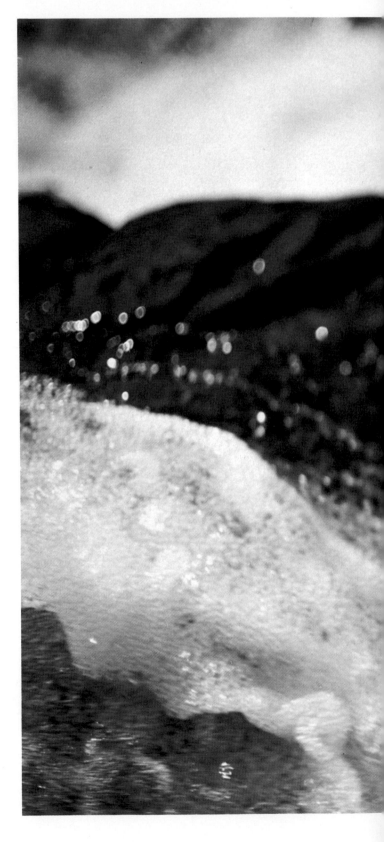

From youth to age I have lived with nature more than with men. In youth I saw nature as a standing invitation to come forth and give play to myself; the streams were for fishing and swimming, the woods were for hunting and exploring, and for all kinds of sylvan adventure; the fields were for berries and birds' nests, and color, and the delight of the world of grasses; the mountains were for climbing and the prospects and the triumphs of their summits.

The world was good; it tasted good, it delighted all my senses. The seasons came and went, each with its own charms and enticements. I was ready for each and contented with each. The spring was for the delights of sugar-making, and the returning birds—the naked maple woods flooded with the warm, creative sunshine, the brown fields slipping off their covering of snow, the loosened rills, the first robin, the first phoebe, the first song sparrow—how all these things thrilled one! The summer was for bare feet, light clothes, freedom from school, strawberries, trout, haymaking, and the Fourth of July. Autumn was for apples, nuts, wild pigeons, gray squirrels, and the great dreamy tranquil days; winter for the fireside, school, games, coasting, and the tonic of frost and snow. How the stars twinkled in winter! how the ice sang and whooped on the ponds! how the snow sculpturing decked all the farm fences! how the sheeted winds stalked across the hills!

Oh, the eagerness and freshness of youth! How the boy enjoys his food, his sleep, his sports, his companions, his truant days! His life is an adventure, he is widening his outlook, he is extending his dominion, he is conquering his kingdom. How cheap are his pleasures, how ready his enthusiasms! In boyhood I have had more delight on a haymow

Blessed is he whose youth was passed upon the farm, and if it was a dairy farm, his memories will be all the more fragrant. The driving of the cows to and from the pasture, every day and every season for years—how much of summer and of nature he got into him on these journeys! What rambles and excursions did this errand furnish the excuse for! The birds and birds' nests, the berries, the squirrels, the woodchucks, the beech woods with their treasures into which the cows loved so to wander and to browse, the fragrant wintergreens and a hundred nameless adventures, all strung upon that brief journey of a half mile to and from the remote pastures. Sometimes a cow or two will be missing when the herd is brought home at night; then to hunt them up is another adventure. My grandfather went out one night to look up an absentee from the yard, when he heard something in the brush, and out stepped a bear into the path before him.

Every Sunday morning the cows were salted. The farm boy would take a pail with three or four quarts of coarse salt, and, followed by the eager herd, go to the field and deposit the salt in handfuls upon smooth stones and rocks and upon clean places on the turf. If you want to know how good salt is, see a cow eat it. She gives the true saline smack. How she dwells upon it, and gnaws the sward and licks the stones where it has been deposited! The cow is the most delightful feeder among animals. It makes one's mouth water to see her eat pumpkins, and to see her at a pile of apples is distracting. How she sweeps off the delectable grass! The sound of her grazing is appetizing; the grass betrays all its sweetness and succulency in parting under her sickle. . . .

Sheep love high, cool, breezy lands. Their range is generally much above that of cattle. Their sharp noses will find picking where a

cow would fare poorly indeed. Hence most farmers utilize their high, wild, and mountain lands by keeping a small flock of sheep. But they are the outlaws of the farm and are seldom within bounds. They make many lively expeditions for the farm boy—driving them out of mischief, hunting them up in the mountains, or salting them on the breezy hills. Then there is the annual sheep-washing, when on a warm day in May or early June the whole herd is driven a mile or more to a suitable pool in the creek, and one by one doused and washed and rinsed in the water. We used to wash below an old gristmill, and it was a pleasing spectacle—the mill, the dam, the overhanging rocks and trees, the round, deep pool, and the huddled and frightened sheep.

Signs and Seasons

When the farmers made "bees," as they did a generation or two ago much more than they do now, a picturesque element was added. There was the stone bee, the husking bee, the "raising," the "moving," etc. When the carpenters had got the timbers of the house or the barn ready, and the foundation was prepared, then the neighbors for miles about were invited to come to the "raisin'." The afternoon was the time chosen. The forenoon was occupied by the carpenter and the farm hands in putting the sills and "sleepers" in place ("sleepers," what a good name for those rude hewn timbers that lie under the floor in the darkness and silence!). When the hands arrived, the great beams and posts and joists and braces were carried to their place on the platform, and the first "bent," as it was called, was put together and pinned by oak pins that the boys brought. Then pike poles were distributed, the men, fifteen or twenty of them, arranged in a line abreast of the bent; the boss carpenter steadied and guided the corner post and gave the word of command—"Take holt, boys!" "Now, set her up!" "Up with her!" "Up she goes!" When it gets shoulder high, it becomes heavy, and there is a pause. The pikes are brought into requisition; every man gets a good hold and braces himself, and waits for the words. "All together now!" shouts the captain; "Heave her up!" "He-o-he!" (heave-all—heave), "he-o-he," at the top of his voice, every man doing his best. Slowly the great timbers go up; louder grows the word of command, till the bent is up. Then it is plumbed and stay-lathed, and another is put together and raised in the same way, till they are all up. Then comes the putting on the great plates—timbers that run lengthwise of the building and match the sills below. Then, if there is time, the putting up of the rafters.

In every neighborhood there was always some man who was especially useful at "raisin's." He was bold and strong and quick. He helped guide and superintend the work. He was the first one up on the bent, catching a pin or a brace and putting it in place. He walked the lofty and perilous plate with the great beetle in hand, put the pins in the holes, and swinging the heavy instrument through the air, drove the pins home. He was as much at home up there as a squirrel....

Then the moving was an event, too. A farmer had a barn to move, or wanted to build a new house on the site of the old one, and the latter must be drawn to one side. Now this work is done with pulleys and rollers by a few men and a horse; then the building was drawn by sheer bovine strength. Every man that had a yoke of cattle in the country round about was invited to assist. The barn or house was pried up and great runners, cut in the woods, placed under it, and under the runners were placed skids. To these runners it was securely chained and pinned; then the cattle—stags,

steers, and oxen, in two long lines, one at each runner—were hitched fast, and, while men and boys aided with great levers, the word to go was given. Slowly the two lines of bulky cattle straightened and settled into their bows; the big chains that wrapped the runners tightened, a dozen or more "gads" were flourished, a dozen or more lusty throats urged their teams at the top of their voices, when there was a creak or a groan as the building stirred. Then the drivers redoubled their efforts; there was a perfect Babel of discordant sounds; the oxen bent to the work, their eyes bulged, their nostrils distended; the lookers-on cheered, and away went the old house or barn as nimbly as a boy on a hand-sled. Not always, however; sometimes the chains would break, or one runner strike a rock, or bury itself in the earth. There were generally enough mishaps or delays to make it interesting.

Signs and Seasons

When the produce of the farm was taken a long distance to market—that was an event, too; the carrying away of the butter in the fall, for instance, to the river, a journey that occupied both ways four days. Then the family marketing was done in a few groceries. Some cloth, new caps and boots for the boys, and a dress, or a shawl, or a cloak for the girls were brought back, besides news and adventure, and strange tidings of the distant world. The farmer was days in getting ready to start; food was prepared and put in a box to stand him on the journey, so as to lessen the hotel expenses, and oats were put up for the horses. The butter was loaded up overnight, and in the cold November morning, long before it was light, he was up and off. I seem to hear the wagon yet, its slow rattle over the frozen ground diminishing in the distance. On the fourth day toward night all grew expectant of his return, but it was usually dark before his wagon was heard coming down the hill, or his voice from before the door summoning a light. When the boys got big enough, one after the other accompanied him each year, until all had made the famous journey and seen the great river and the steamboats, and the thousand and one marvels of the far-away town. When it came my turn to go, I was in a great state of excitement for a week beforehand, for fear my clothes would not be ready, or else that it would be too cold, or else that the world would come to an end before the time fixed for starting. The day previous I roamed the woods in quest of game to supply my bill of fare on the way, and was lucky enough to shoot a

partridge and an owl, though the latter I did not take. Perched high on a "springboard" I made the journey, and saw more sights and wonders than I have ever seen on a journey since, or ever expect to again.

Signs and Seasons

Sometimes the threshing was done in the open air, upon a broad rock, or a smooth, dry plat of greensward;.... The flail makes a louder *thud* in the fields than you would imagine; and in the splendid October weather it is a pleasing spectacle to behold the gathering of the ruddy crop, and three or four little figures beating out the grain with their flails in some sheltered nook, or some grassy lane lined with cedars. When there are three flails beat-

ing together, it makes lively music; and when there are four, they follow each other so fast that it is a continuous roll of sound, and it requires a very steady stroke not to hit or get hit by the others. There is just room and time to get your blow in, and that is all. When one flail is upon the straw, another has just left it, another is halfway down, and the fourth is high and straight in the air. It is like a swiftly revolving wheel that delivers four blows at each revolution. Threshing, like mowing, goes much easier in company than when alone; yet many a farmer or laborer spends nearly all the late fall and winter days shut in the barn, pounding doggedly upon the endless sheaves of oats and rye.

Signs and Seasons

23

One of the features of farm life peculiar to this country, and one of the most picturesque of them all, is sugar-making in the maple woods in spring. This is the first work of the season, and to the boys is more play than work. In the Old World, and in more simple and imaginative times, how such an occupation as this would have got into literature, and how many legends and associations would have clustered around it! It is woodsy, and savors of the trees; it is an encampment among the maples. Before the bud swells, before the grass springs, before the plow is started, comes the sugar harvest. It is the sequel of the bitter frost; a sap-run is the sweet good-by of winter. It denotes a certain equipoise of the season; the heat of the day fully balances the frost of the night. In New York and New England, the time of the sap hovers about the vernal equinox, beginning a week or ten days before, and continuing a week or ten days after. As the days and nights get equal, the heat and cold get equal, and the sap mounts. A day that brings the bees out of the hive will bring the sap out of the maple tree. It is the fruit of the equal marriage of the sun and the frost. When the frost is all out of the ground, and all the snow gone from its surface, the flow stops. The thermometer must not rise above 38° or 40° by day, or sink below 24° or 25° at night, with wind in the northwest....

In my sugar-making days, the sap was carried to the boiling place in pails by the aid of a neck yoke and stored in hogsheads, and boiled or evaporated in immense kettles or caldrons set in huge stone arches; now, the hogshead goes to the trees hauled upon a sled by a team, and the sap is evaporated in broad, shallow, sheet-iron pans—a great saving of fuel and of labor.

Many a farmer sits up all night boiling his sap, when the run has been an extra good one, and a lone vigil he has of it amid the silent trees and beside his wild hearth. If he has a sap-house, as is now so common, he may make himself fairly comfortable; and if a companion, he may have a good time or a glorious wake.

Signs and Seasons

Trout streams coursed through every valley my boyhood knew. I crossed them, and was often lured and detained by them, on my way to and from school. We bathed in them during the long summer noons, and felt for the trout under their banks. A holiday was a holiday indeed that brought permission to go fishing over on Rose's Brook, or up Hardscrabble, or in Meeker's Hollow; all-day trips, from morning till night, through meadows and pastures and beechen woods, wherever the shy, limpid stream led. What an appetite it developed! a hunger that was fierce and aboriginal, and that the wild strawberries we plucked as we crossed the hill teased rather than allayed. When but a few hours could be had, gained perhaps by doing some piece of work about the farm or garden in half the allotted time, the little creek that headed in the paternal domain was handy; when half a day was at one's disposal, there were the hemlocks, less than a mile distant, with their loitering, meditative, log-impeded stream and their dusky, fragrant depths. Alert and wide-eyed, one picked his way along, startled now and then by the sudden bursting-up of the partridge, or by the whistling wings of the "dropping snipe," pressing through the brush and the briers, or finding an easy passage over the trunk of a prostrate tree, carefully letting his hook down through some tangle into a still pool, or standing in some high, sombre avenue and watching his line float in and out amid the moss-covered boulders.

Locusts and Wild Honey

25

In March that brief summary of a bear, the raccoon, comes out of his den in the ledges, and leaves his sharp digitigrade track upon the snow—traveling not unfrequently in pairs—a lean, hungry couple, bent on pillage and plunder. They have an unenviable time of it—feasting in the summer and fall, hibernating in winter, and starving in spring. In April I have found the young of the previous year creeping about the fields, so reduced by starvation as to be quite helpless, and offering no resistance to my taking them up by the tail and carrying them home.

Winter Sunshine

A "sap-run" seldom lasts more than two or three days. By that time there is a change in the weather, perhaps a rainstorm, which takes the frost nearly all out of the ground. Then, before there can be another run, the trees must be wound up again, the storm must have a white tail, and "come off" cold. Presently the sun rises clear again, and cuts the snow or softens the hard-frozen ground with his beams, and the trees take a fresh start. The boys go through the wood, emptying out the buckets or the pans, and reclaiming those that have blown away, and the delightful work is

resumed. But the first run, like first love, is always the best, always the fullest, always the sweetest; while there is a purity and delicacy of flavor about the sugar that far surpasses any subsequent yield....

I think any person who has tried it will agree with me about the charm of sugar making, though he have no tooth for the sweet itself. It is enough that it is the first spring work, and takes one to the woods. The robins are just arriving, and their merry calls ring through the glades. The squirrels are now venturing out, and the woodpeckers and nuthatches run briskly up the trees. The crow begins to caw, with his accustomed heartiness and assurance; and one sees the white rump and golden shafts of the high-hole [yellow-shafted flicker] as he flits about the open woods. Next week, or the week after, it may be time to begin plowing, and other sober work about the farm; but this week we will picnic among the maples, and our campfire shall be an incense to spring.

Winter Sunshine

There is a brief period in our spring when I like more than at any other time to drive along the country roads, or even to be shot along by steam and have the landscape presented to me like a map. It is at that period, usually late in April, when we behold the first quickening of the earth. The waters have subsided, the roads have become dry, the sunshine has grown strong and its warmth has penetrated the sod; there is a stir of preparation about the farm and all through the country. One does not care to see things very closely; his interest in nature is not special but general. The earth is coming to life again. All the genial and more fertile places in the landscape are brought out; the earth is quickened in spots and streaks; you can see at a glance where man and nature have dealt the most kindly with it. The warm, moist places, the places that have had the wash of some building or of the road, or have been subjected to some special mellowing influence, how quickly the turf awakens there and shows the tender green! See what the landscape would be, how much earlier spring would come to it, if every square yard of it were alike moist and fertile. As the later snows lay in patches here and there, so now the earliest verdure is irregularly spread over the landscape, and is especially marked on certain slopes, as if it had blown over from the other side and lodged there.

A little earlier the homesteads looked cold and naked; the old farmhouse was bleak and unattractive; now Nature seems especially to smile upon it; her genial influences crowd up around it; the turf awakens all about as if in the spirit of friendliness. See the old barn on the meadow slope; the green seems to have oozed out from it, and to have flowed slowly down the hill; at a little distance it is lost in the sere stubble. One can see where every spring lies buried about the fields; its influence is felt at the surface, and the turf is early quickened there. Where the cattle have loved to lie and ruminate in the warm summer twilight, there the April sunshine loves to linger too, till the sod thrills to new life. . . .

The full charm of this April landscape is not brought out till the afternoon. It seems to need the slanting rays of the evening sun to give it the right mellowness and tenderness, or the right perspective. It is, perhaps, a little too bald in the strong, white light of the earlier part of the day; but when the faint, four-o'clock shadows begin to come out, and we look through the green vistas, and along the farm lanes toward the west, or out across long stretches of fields above which spring seems fairly hovering, just ready to alight, and note the teams slowly plowing, the brightened mould-board gleaming in the sun now and then—it is at such times we feel its fresh, delicate attraction the most. There is no foliage on the trees yet; only here and there the red bloom of the soft maple, illuminated by the declining sun, shows vividly against the tender green of a slope beyond, or a willow, like a thin veil, stands out against a leafless wood. Here and there a little meadow watercourse is golden with marsh marigolds, or some fence border, or rocky streak of neglected pasture land, is thickly starred with the white flowers of the bloodroot. The eye can devour a succession of landscapes at such a time; there is nothing that sates or entirely fills it, but every spring token stimulates it and makes it more on the alert.

Signs and Seasons

In my walks in April, I am on the lookout for watercresses. It is a plant that has the pungent April flavor. In many parts of the country the watercress seems to have become completely naturalized, and is essentially a wild plant. I found it one day in a springy place, on the top of a high, wooded mountain, far from human habitation. We gathered it and ate it with our sandwiches. Where the walker cannot find this salad, a good substitute may be had in our

This lady's slipper is one of the rarest and choicest of our wild flowers, and its haunts and its beauty are known only to the few. Those who have the secret guard it closely, lest their favorite be exterminated. A well-known botanist in one of the large New England cities told me that it was found in but one place in that neighborhood, and that the secret, so far as he knew, was known to but three persons, and was carefully kept by them....

Report had come to me, through my botanizing neighbor, that in a certain quaking sphagnum bog in the woods the showy lady's slipper could be found. The locality proved to be the marrowy grave of an extinct lake or black tarn. On the borders of it the white azalea was in bloom, fast fading. In the midst of it were spruces and black ash and giant ferns, and, low in the spongy, mossy bottom, the pitcher plant. The lady's slipper grew in little groups and companies all about. Never have I beheld a prettier sight—so gay, so festive, so holiday-looking.

Riverby

One sometimes seems to discover a familiar wild flower anew by coming upon it in some peculiar and striking situation. Our columbine is at all times and in all places one of the most exquisitely beautiful of flowers; yet one spring day, when I saw it growing out of a small seam on the face of a great lichen-covered wall of rock, where no soil or mould was visible—a jet of foliage and color shooting out of a black line on the face of a perpendicular mountain wall and rising up like a tiny fountain, its drops turning to flame-colored jewels that hung and danced in the air against the gray rocky surface—its beauty became something magical and audacious.

Riverby

On looking at the southern and more distant Catskills from the Hudson River on the east, or on looking at them from the west from some point of vantage in Delaware County, you see, amid the group of mountains, one that looks like the back and shoulders of a gigantic horse. The horse has got his head down grazing; the shoulders are high, and the descent from them down his neck very steep; if he were to lift up his head, one sees that it would be carried far above all other peaks, and that the noble beast might gaze straight to his peers in the Adiron-

great haste, and ran up the cellar wall and along its top till they came to a floor timber that stopped their progress, when they turned at bay, and looked excitedly back along the course they had come. In a moment a weasel, evidently in hot pursuit of them, came out of the hole, and, seeing the farmer, checked his course and darted back. The rats had doubtless turned to give him fight, and would probably have been a match for him.

Signs and Seasons

In most of the eastern counties of the state, the interest and profit of the farm revolve about the cow. The dairy is the one great matter—for milk, when milk can be shipped to the New York market, and for butter when it cannot. Great barns and stables and milking sheds, and immense meadows and cattle on a thousand hills, are the prominent agricultural features of these sections of the country. Good grass and good water are the two indispensables to successful dairying. And the two generally go together. Where there are plenty of copious cold springs, there is no dearth of grass. When the cattle are compelled to browse upon weeds and various wild growths, the milk and butter will betray it in the flavor. Tender, juicy grass, the ruddy blossoming clover, or the fragrant, well-cured hay, make the delicious milk and the sweet butter. Then there is a charm about a natural pastoral country that belongs to no other. Go through Orange County in May and see the vivid emerald of the smooth fields and hills. It is a new experience of the beauty and effectiveness of simple grass. And this grass has rare virtues, too, and imparts a flavor to the milk and butter that has made them famous.

Along all the sources of the Delaware the land flows with milk, if not with honey. The grass is excellent, except in times of protracted drought, and then the browsings in the beech and birch woods are a good substitute. Butter is the staple product. Every housewife is or wants to be a famous butter-maker, and Delaware County butter rivals that of Orange in market. Delaware is a high, cool grazing country. The farms lie tilted up against the sides of the mountain or lapping over the hills, striped or checked with stone walls, and presenting to the eye long stretches of pasture and meadow land, alternating with plowed fields and patches of waving grain. Few of their features are picturesque; they are bare, broad, and simple. The farmhouse gets itself a coat of white paint, and green blinds to the windows, and the barn and wagon house a coat of red paint with white trimmings, as soon as possible. A penstock flows by the doorway, rows of tin pans sun themselves in the yard, and the great wheel of the churning machine flanks the milk house, or rattles behind it. The winters are severe, the snow deep. The principal fuel is still wood—beech, birch, and maple. It is hauled off the mountain in great logs when the first November or December snows come, and cut up and piled in the wood houses and under a shed. Here the axe still rules the winter, and it may be heard all day and every day upon the woodpile, or echoing through the frostbound wood, the coat of the chopper hanging to a limb, and his white chips strewing the snow.

Signs and Seasons

When I want the wild of a little different flavor and quality from that immediately about my cabin, I go a mile through the woods to Black Creek, here called the Shattega, and put my canoe into a long, smooth, silent stretch of water that winds through a heavily timbered marsh till it leads into Black Pond, an oval sheet of water half a mile or more across.

The squirrel would shoot up the tree, making only a brown streak from the bottom to the top; would seize his nut and rush down again in the most precipitate manner. Halfway to his den, which was not over three rods distant, he would rush up the trunk of another tree for a few yards to make an observation. No danger being near, he would dive into his den and reappear again in a twinkling.

Returning for another nut, he would mount the second tree again for another observation. Satisfied that the coast was clear, he would spin along the top of the ground to the tree that bore the nuts, shoot up it as before, seize the fruit, and then back again to his retreat.

Never did he fail during the half hour or more that I watched him to take an observation on his way both to and from his nest. It was "snatch and run" with him. Something seemed to say to him all the time: "Look out! look out!" "The cat!" "The hawk!" "The owl!" "The boy with the gun!"

It was a bleak December morning; the first fine flakes of a cold, driving snowstorm were

After a storm, ice forms a transparent coat over the trees' bare branches. The woods became a lacy tangle of twigs.

just beginning to sift down, and the squirrel was eager to finish harvesting his nuts in time. It was quite touching to see how hurried and anxious and nervous he was. I felt like going out and lending a hand. The nuts were small, poor pig-nuts, and I thought of all the gnawing he would have to do to get at the scanty meat they held.

Riverby

A fall of snow, and this icy uproar [Hudson River] is instantly hushed, the river sleeps in peace. The snow is like a coverlid, which protects the ice from the changes of temperature of the air, and brings repose to its uneasy spirit.

A dweller upon its banks, I am an interested spectator of the spring and winter harvests which its waters yield. In the stern winter nights, it is a pleasant thought that a harvest is growing down there on those desolate plains which will bring work to many needy hands by and by, and health and comfort to the great cities some months later. When the nights are coldest, the ice grows as fast as corn in July. It is a crop that usually takes two or three weeks to grow, and, if the water is very roily or brackish, even longer. Men go out from time to time and examine it, as the farmer goes out and examines his grain or grass, to see when it will do to cut. If there comes a deep fall of snow before the ice has attained much thickness, it is "pricked," so as to let the water up through and form snow-ice. A band of fifteen or twenty men, about a yard apart, each armed with a chisel-bar and marching in line, puncture the ice at each step with a single sharp thrust. To and fro they go, leaving a belt behind them that presently becomes saturated with water. But ice, to be first quality, must grow from beneath, not from above. It is a crop quite as uncertain as any other. A good yield every two or three years, as they say of wheat out West, is about all that can be counted

upon. When there is an abundant harvest, after the icehouses are filled, they stack great quantities of it, as the farmer stacks his surplus hay.

The cutting and gathering of the ice enlivens these broad, white, desolate fields amazingly. One looks down upon the busy scene as from a hilltop upon a river meadow in haying time, only here the figures stand out much more sharply than they do from a summer meadow. There is the broad, straight, blue-black canal emerging into view, and running nearly across the river; this is the highway that lays open the farm. On either side lie the fields or ice-meadows, each marked out by cedar or hemlock boughs. The farther one is cut first, and, when cleared, shows a large, long, black parallelogram in the midst of the plain of snow. Then the next one is cut, leaving a strip or tongue of ice between the two for the horses to move and turn upon. Sometimes nearly two hundred men and boys, with numerous horses, are at work at once, marking, plowing, planing, scraping, sawing, hauling, chiseling; some floating down the pond on great square islands towed by a horse, or their fellow workmen; others distributed along the canal, bending to their ice hooks; others upon the bridges, separating the blocks with their chisel-bars; others feeding the elevators; ....

A beautiful phenomenon may at times be witnessed on the river in the morning after a night of extreme cold. The new black ice is found to be covered with a sudden growth of frost ferns—exquisite fernlike formations from a half inch to an inch in length, standing singly and in clusters, and under the morning sun presenting a most novel appearance. They impede the skate, and are presently broken down and blown about by the wind.

The scenes and doings of summer are counterfeited in other particulars upon these crystal plains. Some bright, breezy day you casually glance down the river and behold a sail—a sail like that of a pleasure yacht of summer. Is the river open again below there? is your first half-defined inquiry. But with what unwonted speed the sail is moving across the view! Before you have fairly drawn another breath it has turned, unperceived, and is shooting with equal swiftness in the opposite direction. Who ever saw such a lively sail! It does not bend before the breeze, but darts to and fro as if it moved in a vacuum, or like a shadow over a screen. Then you remember the iceboats, and you open your eyes to the fact. Another and another come into view around the elbow, turning and flashing in the sun, and hurtling across each other's path like white-winged gulls. They turn so quickly, and dash off again at such speed, that they produce the illusion of something singularly light and intangible. In fact, an iceboat is a sort of disembodied yacht; it is a sail on skates. The only semblance to a boat is the sail and the rudder. The platform under which the skates or runners—three in number—are rigged is broad and low; upon this the pleasure-seekers, wrapped in their furs or blankets, lie at full length, and, looking under the sail, skim the frozen surface with their eyes. The speed attained is sometimes very great—more than a mile per minute, and sufficient to carry them ahead of the fastest express train. When going at this rate the boat will leap like a greyhound, and thrilling stories are told of the fearful crevasses, or open places in the ice, that are cleared at a bound. And yet withal she can be brought up to the wind so suddenly as to shoot the unwary occupants off, and send them skating on their noses some yards.

Signs and Seasons

One season, the last day of December was very warm. The bees were out of the hive, and there was no frost in the air or in the ground. I was walking in the woods, when as I paused in the shade of a hemlock tree I heard a sound proceed from beneath the wet leaves on the ground but a few feet from me that suggested a frog. Following it cautiously up, I at last determined upon the exact spot from whence the sound issued; lifting up the thick layer of leaves, there sat a frog—the wood frog, one of the first to appear in the marshes in spring, and which I have elsewhere called the "clucking frog"—in a little excavation in the surface of the leaf mould. As it sat there the top of its back was level with the surface of the ground. This, then, was its hibernaculum; here it was prepared to pass the winter, with only a coverlid of wet matted leaves between it and zero weather. Forthwith I set up as a prophet of warm weather, and among other things predicted a failure of the ice crop on the river; which, indeed, others, who had not heard frogs croak on the 31st of December, had also begun to predict. Surely, I thought, this frog knows what it is about; here is the wisdom of nature; it would have gone deeper into the ground than that if a severe winter was approaching; so I was not anxious about my coal bin, nor disturbed by longings for Florida. But what a winter followed, the winter of 1885, when the Hudson became coated with ice nearly two feet thick, and when March was as cold as January! I thought of my frog under the hemlock and wondered how it was faring. So one day the latter part of March, when the snow was gone, and there was a feeling of spring in the air, I turned aside in my walk to investigate it. The matted leaves were still frozen hard, but I succeeded in lifting them up and exposing the frog. There it sat as fresh and unscathed as in the fall. The ground beneath and all about it was still frozen like a rock, but apparently it had some means of its own of

resisting the frost. It winked and bowed its head when I touched it, but did not seem inclined to leave its retreat. Some days later, after the frost was nearly all out of the ground, I passed that way, and found my frog had come out of its seclusion and was resting amid the dry leaves.

Signs and Seasons

The snow-walkers are mostly night-walkers also, and the record they leave upon the snow is the main clew one has to their life and doings. The hare is nocturnal in its habits, and though a very lively creature at night, with regular courses and runways through the wood, is entirely quiet by day. Timid as he is, he makes little effort to conceal himself, usually squatting beside a log, stump, or tree, and seeming to avoid rocks and ledges where he might be partially housed from the cold and the snow, but where also—and this consideration undoubtedly determines his choice—he would be more apt to fall a prey to his enemies. In this, as well as in many other respects, he differs from the rabbit proper: he never burrows in the ground, or takes refuge in a den or hole, when pursued. If caught in the open fields, he is much confused and easily overtaken by the dog; but in the woods, he leaves him at a bound. In summer, when first disturbed, he beats the ground violently with his feet, by which means he would express to you his surprise or displeasure; it is a dumb way he has of scolding. After leaping a few yards, he pauses an instant, as if to determine the degree of danger, and then hurries away with a much lighter tread. . . .

He abounds in dense woods, preferring localities filled with a small undergrowth of beech and birch, upon the bark of which he feeds. Nature is rather partial to him, and matches his extreme local habits and character with a suit that corresponds with his surroundings—reddish gray in summer and white in winter.

The sharp-rayed track of the partridge adds another figure to this fantastic embroidery upon the winter snow. Her course is a clear, strong line, sometimes quite wayward, but generally very direct, steering for the densest, most impenetrable places—leading you over logs and through brush, alert and expectant, till, suddenly, she bursts up a few yards from you, and goes humming through the trees—the complete triumph of endurance and vigor. Hardy native bird, may your tracks never be fewer, or your visits to the birch tree less frequent! . . .

In February another track appears upon the snow, slender and delicate, about a third larger than that of the gray squirrel, indicating no haste or speed, but, on the contrary, denoting the most imperturbable ease and leisure, the footprints so close together that the trail appears like a chain of curiously carved links. Sir *Mephitis mephitica*, or, in plain English, the skunk, has awakened from his six weeks' nap, and come out into society again. He is a nocturnal traveler, very bold and impudent, coming quite up to the barn and outbuildings, and sometimes taking up his quarters for the season under the haymow. There is no such word as hurry in his dictionary, as you may see by his path upon the snow. He has a very sneaking, insinuating way, and goes creeping about the fields and woods, never once in a perceptible degree altering his gait, and, if a fence crosses his course, steers for a break or opening to avoid climbing. He is too indolent even to dig his own hole, but appropriates that of a woodchuck, or hunts out a crevice in the rocks, from which he extends his rambling in

all directions, preferring damp, thawy weather. He has very little discretion or cunning, and holds a trap in utter contempt, stepping into it as soon as beside it, relying implicitly for defense against all forms of danger upon the unsavory punishment he is capable of inflicting. He is quite indifferent to both man and beast, and will not hurry himself to get out of the way of either. Walking through the summer fields at twilight, I have come near stepping upon him, and was much the more disturbed of the two. When attacked in the open field he confounds the plans of his enemies by the unheard-of tactics of exposing his rear rather than his front. "Come if you dare," he says, and his attitude makes even the farm dog pause. After a few encounters of this kind, and if you entertain the usual hostility towards him, your mode of attack will speedily resolve itself into moving about him in a circle, the radius of which will be the exact distance at which you can hurl a stone with accuracy and effect.

He has a secret to keep and knows it, and is careful not to betray himself until he can do so with the most telling effect. I have known him to preserve his serenity even when caught in a steel trap, and look the very picture of injured innocence, maneuvering carefully and deliberately to extricate his foot from the grasp of the naughty jaws. Do not by any means take pity on him, and lend a helping hand!

How pretty his face and head! How fine and delicate his teeth, like a weasel's or a cat's! When about a third grown, he looks so well that one covets him for a pet. He is quite precocious, however, and capable, even at this tender age, of making a very strong appeal to your sense of smell. . . .

The secretion upon which he relies for defense, and which is the chief source of his unpopularity, while it affords good reasons against cultivating him as a pet, and mars his

attractiveness as game, is by no means the greatest indignity that can be offered to a nose. It is a rank, living smell, and has none of the sickening qualities of disease or putrefaction. Indeed, I think a good smeller will enjoy its most refined intensity. It approaches the sublime, and makes the nose tingle. It is tonic and bracing, and, I can readily believe, has rare medicinal qualities.

Winter Sunshine

The red fox is the sportsman's prize, and the only fur bearer worthy of note in these mountains. I go out in the morning, after a fresh fall of snow, and see at all points where he has crossed the road. Here he has leisurely passed within rifle range of the house, evidently reconnoitering the premises with an eye to the hen-roost. That clear, sharp track—there is no mistaking it for the clumsy footprint of a little dog. All his wildness and agility are photographed in it. Here he has taken fright, or suddenly recollected an engagement, and in long, graceful leaps, barely touching the fence, has gone careering up the hill as fleet as the wind.

The wild, buoyant creature, how beautiful he is! I had often seen his dead carcass, and at a distance had witnessed the hounds drive him across the upper fields; but the thrill and excitement of meeting him in his wild freedom in the woods were unknown to me till, one cold winter day, drawn thither by the baying of a hound, I stood near the summit of the mountain, waiting a renewal of the sound, that I might determine the course of the dog and choose my position—stimulated by the ambition of all young Nimrods to bag some notable game. Long I waited, and patiently, till, chilled and benumbed, I was about to turn back, when, hearing a slight noise, I looked up and beheld a most superb fox, loping along with inimitable grace and ease, evidently disturbed, but not pursued by the hound, and so absorbed in his private meditations that he failed to see me, though I stood transfixed with amazement and admiration, not ten yards distant. I took his measure at a glance—a large male, with dark legs, and massive tail tipped with white— a most magnificent creature; but so astonished and fascinated was I by this sudden appearance and matchless beauty, that not till I had caught the last glimpse of him, as he disappeared over a knoll, did I awake to my duty as a sportsman, and realize what an opportunity to distinguish myself I had unconsciously let slip. I clutched my gun, half angrily, as if it was to blame, and went home out of humor with myself and all fox-kind. But I have since thought better of the experience, and concluded that I bagged the game after all, the best part of it, and fleeced Reynard of something more valuable than his fur, without his knowledge.

Winter Sunshine

John-of-the-Birds

The piercing stare of the sparrow hawk (opposite) suggests an ever-watchful nature. The ruby-throated hummingbird (above) is as brilliant as his colorful surroundings.

Of all the creatures John Burroughs observed over the many decades of his outdoor wanderings, his favorite were the birds. From the smallest hummingbird whose nest he found in the woods, to the migrating ducks on the ponds and the eagles soaring between the cliffs of the Hudson, birds were a primary part of his life.

His study of them, always in the wild, was so intense that he became known as an expert, regardless of a lack of formal ornithological studies. People unknown to him would send him descriptions of birds they had seen and ask him to identify them. Sometimes the descriptions were incomplete, and Burroughs used the time of the season and the geographical area of the writer to pin down the species. Once he complimented a small boy who had written him, saying it was wonderful that the boy had noticed the bird jumped instead of walked.

As John Muir is sometimes today called John-of-the-Mountains, so Burroughs is sometimes known as John-of-the-Birds. His love for these creatures was strong, and through them he gained a greater understanding of nature as a whole.

Spring in our northern climate may fairly be said to extend from the middle of March to the middle of June. At least, the vernal tide continues to rise until the latter date, and it is not till after the summer solstice that the shoots and twigs begin to harden and turn to wood, or the grass to lose any of its freshness and succulency.

It is this period that marks the return of the birds—one or two of the more hardy or half-domesticated species, like the song sparrow and the bluebird, usually arriving in March, while the rarer and more brilliant wood birds bring up the procession in June. But each stage of the advancing season gives prominence to certain species, as to certain flowers. The dandelion tells me when to look for the swallow, the dogtooth violet when to expect the wood-thrush, and when I have found the wake-robin [trillium] in bloom I know the season is fairly inaugurated. With me this flower is associated, not merely with the awakening of Robin, for he has been awake some weeks, but with the universal awakening and rehabilitation of nature.

Yet the coming and going of the birds is more or less a mystery and a surprise. We go out in the morning, and no thrush or vireo is to be heard; we go out again, and every tree and grove is musical; yet again, and all is silent. Who saw them come? Who saw them depart?

This pert little winter wren, for instance, darting in and out the fence, diving under the rubbish here and coming up yards away—how does he manage with those little circular wings to compass degrees and zones, and arrive always in the nick of time? Last August I saw him in the remotest wilds of the Adirondacks, impatient and inquisitive as usual; a few weeks later, on the Potomac, I was greeted by the same hardy little busybody. Does he travel by easy stages from bush to bush and

"The bluebird is a home bird....
His coming or reappearance in the spring
marks a new chapter in the progress of the
season; things are never quite the same
after one has heard that note."

from wood to wood? Or has that compact little body force and courage to brave the night and the upper air, and so achieve leagues at one pull?

And yonder bluebird with the earth tinge on his breast and the sky tinge on his back—did he come down out of heaven on that bright March morning when he told us so softly and plaintively that, if we pleased, spring had come? Indeed, there is nothing in the return of the birds more curious and suggestive than in the first appearance, or rumors of the appearance, of this little blue-coat. The bird at first seems a mere wandering voice in the air; one hears its call or carol on some bright March morning, but is uncertain of its source or direction; it falls like a drop of rain when no cloud is visible; one looks and listens, but to no purpose. The weather changes, perhaps a cold snap with snow comes on, and it may be a week before I hear the note again, and this time or the next perchance see the bird sitting on a stake in the fence lifting his wing as he calls cheerily to his mate. Its notes now

become daily more frequent; the birds multiply, and, flitting from point to point, call and warble more confidently and gleefully. Their boldness increases till one sees them hovering with a saucy, inquiring air about barns and outbuildings, peeping into dovecotes and stable windows, inspecting knotholes and pump-trees, intent only on a place to nest. They wage war against robins and wrens, pick quarrels with swallows, and seem to deliberate for days over the policy of taking forcible possession of one of the mud-houses of the latter. But as the season advances they drift more into the background. Schemes of conquest which they at first seemed bent upon are abandoned, and they settle down very quietly in their old quarters in remote stumpy fields.

Not long after the bluebird comes the robin, sometimes in March, but in most of the Northern states April is the month of the robin. In large numbers they scour the fields and groves. You hear their piping in the meadow, in the pasture, on the hillside. Walk in the woods, and the dry leaves rustle with the whir of their wings, the air is vocal with their cheery call. In excess of joy and vivacity, they run, leap, scream, chase each other through the air, diving and sweeping among the trees with perilous rapidity.

In that free, fascinating, half-work and half-play pursuit—sugar-making—a pursuit which still lingers in many parts of New York, as in New England—the robin is one's constant companion. When the day is sunny and the ground bare, you meet him at all points and hear him at all hours. At sunset, on the tops of the tall maples, with look heavenward, and in a spirit of utter abandonment, he carols his simple strain. And sitting thus amid the stark, silent trees, above the wet, cold earth, with the chill of winter still in the air, there is no fitter or sweeter songster in the whole round year. It

is in keeping with the scene and the occasion. How round and genuine the notes are, and how eagerly our ears drink them in! The first utterance, and the spell of winter is thoroughly broken, and the remembrance of it afar off.

Robin is one of the most native and democratic of our birds; he is one of the family, and seems much nearer to us than those rare, exotic visitants, as the orchard starling or rose-breasted grosbeak, with their distant, high-bred ways. Hardy, noisy, frolicsome, neighborly, and domestic in his habits, strong of wing and bold in spirit, he is the pioneer of the thrush family, and well worthy of the finer artists whose coming he heralds and in a measure prepares us for.

I could wish Robin less native and plebeian in one respect—the building of his nest. Its coarse material and rough masonry are creditable neither to his skill as a workman nor to his taste as an artist. I am the more forcibly reminded of his deficiency in this respect from observing yonder hummingbird's nest, which is a marvel of fitness and adaptation, a proper setting for this winged gem—the body of it composed of a white, feltlike substance, probably the down of some plant or the wool of some worm, and toned down in keeping with

*Burroughs admired the robin (above) for its cheerful song
and playful antics. The Eastern kingbird (opposite), somewhat smaller
than a robin, is a belligerent protector of its territory.*

the branch on which it sits by minute tree-lichens, woven together by threads as fine and frail as gossamer. From Robin's good looks and musical turn, we might reasonably predict a domicile of equal fitness and elegance. At least I demand of him as clean and handsome a nest as the kingbird's, whose harsh jingle, compared with Robin's evening melody, is as the clatter of pots and kettles beside the tone of a flute. I love his note and ways better even than those of the orchard starling or the Baltimore oriole; yet his nest, compared with theirs, is a half-subterranean hut contrasted with a Roman villa. There is something courtly and poetical in a pensile nest. Next to a castle in the air is a dwelling suspended to the slender branch of a tall tree, swayed and rocked forever by the wind. Why need wings be afraid of falling? Why build only where boys can

climb? After all, we must set it down to the account of Robin's democratic turn: he is no aristocrat, but one of the people; and therefore we should expect stability in his workmanship, rather than elegance.

Another April bird, which makes her appearance sometimes earlier and sometimes later than Robin, and whose memory I fondly cherish, is the phoebe bird, the pioneer of the flycatchers. In the inland farming districts, I used to notice her, on some bright morning about Easter Day, proclaiming her arrival, with much variety of motion and attitude, from the peak of the barn or hayshed. As yet, you may have heard only the plaintive, homesick note of the bluebird, or the faint trill of the song sparrow; and Phoebe's clear, vivacious assurance of her veritable bodily presence among us again is welcomed by all ears. At

agreeable intervals in her lay she describes a circle or an ellipse in the air, ostensibly prospecting for insects, but really, I suspect, as an artistic flourish, thrown in to make up in some way for the deficiency of her musical performance. If plainness of dress indicates powers of song, as it usually does, then Phoebe ought to be unrivaled in musical ability, for surely that ashen-gray suit is the superlative of plainness; and that form, likewise, would hardly pass for a "perfect figure" of a bird. The seasonableness of her coming, however, and her civil, neighborly ways, shall make up for all deficiencies in song and plumage. After a few weeks Phoebe is seldom seen, except as she darts from her moss-covered nest beneath some bridge or shelving cliff.

Another April comer, who arrives shortly after Robin redbreast, with whom he associates both at this season and in the autumn, is the gold-winged woodpecker, alias "high-hole," alias [yellow-shafted] "flicker," alias "yarup." He is an old favorite of my boyhood, and his note to me means very much. He announces his arrival by a long, loud call, repeated from the dry branch of some tree, or a stake in the fence—a thoroughly melodious April sound.

Wake-Robin

The simple art of the bird consists in choosing common, neutral-tinted material, as moss, dry leaves, twigs, and various odds and ends, and placing the structure on a convenient branch, where it blends in color with its surroundings; but how consummate is this art, and how skillfully is the nest concealed! We occasionally light upon it, but who, unaided by the movements of the bird, could find it out? During the present season I went to the woods nearly every day for a fortnight without making any discoveries of this kind, till one day, paying them a farewell visit, I chanced to come upon several nests. A black and white creeping warbler [brown creeper] suddenly became much alarmed as I approached a crumbling old stump in a dense part of the forest. He alighted upon it, chirped sharply, ran up and down its sides, and finally left it with much reluctance. The nest, which contained three young birds nearly fledged, was placed upon the ground, at the foot of the stump, and in such a position that the color of the young harmonized perfectly with the bits of bark, sticks, etc., lying about. My eye rested upon them for the second time before I made them out. They hugged the nest very closely, but as I put down my hand they all scampered off with loud cries for help, which caused the parent birds to place themselves almost within my reach. The nest was merely a little dry grass arranged in a thick bed of dry leaves.

Wake-Robin

A lady once asked me if there was any individuality among the birds, or if those of the same kind were as near alike as two peas. I was obliged to answer that to the eye those of the same species *were* as near alike as two peas, but that in their songs there were often marks of originality. Caged or domesticated birds develop notes and traits of their own, and among the more familiar orchard and garden birds one may notice the same tendency. I observe a great variety of songs, and even qualities of voice, among the orioles and among the song sparrows. On this trip my ear was especially attracted to some striking and original sparrow songs. At one point I was half afraid I had let pass an opportunity to identify a new warbler, but finally concluded it was a song sparrow. On another occasion I used to hear day after day a sparrow that appeared to have some organic defect in its voice: part of its song was scarcely above a whisper, as if the bird was suffering from a very bad cold. I have heard a bobolink and a hermit thrush with similar defects of voice. I have heard a robin with a part of the whistle of the quail in his song. It was out of time and out of tune, but the robin seemed insensible of the incongruity, and sang as loudly and as joyously as any of his mates. A catbird will sometimes show a special genius for mimicry, and I have known one to suggest very plainly some notes of the bobolink.

Pepacton

It is not generally known that individual birds of the same species show different degrees of musical ability. This is often noticed in caged birds, among which the principle of variation seems more active; but an attentive observer notes the same fact in wild birds. Occasionally he hears one that in powers of song surpasses all its fellows. I have heard a sparrow, an oriole, and a wood thrush, each of which had a song of its own that far exceeded any other. I stood one day by a trout stream, and suspended my fishing for several minutes to watch a song sparrow that was singing on a dry limb before me. He had five distinct songs, each as markedly different from the others as any human songs, which he repeated one after the other. He may have had a sixth or a seventh, but he bethought himself of some business in the next field, and flew away before he had exhausted his repertory. I once had a letter from Robert Louis Stevenson, who said he had

read an account I had written of the song of the English blackbird. He said I might as well talk of the song of man; that every blackbird had its own song; and then he told me of a remarkable singer he used to hear somewhere amid the Scottish hills. But his singer was, of course, an exception; twenty-four blackbirds out of every twenty-five probably sing the same song, with no appreciable variations: but the twenty-fifth may show extraordinary powers. I told Stevenson that his famous singer had probably been to school to some nightingale on the Continent or in southern England. I might have told him of the robin I once heard here that sang with great spirit and

accuracy the song of the brown thrasher, or of another that had the note of the whip-poor-will interpolated in the regular robin song, or of still another that had the call of the quail.

Ways of Nature

A man has a sharper eye than a dog, or a fox, or than any of the wild creatures, but not so sharp an ear or nose. But in the birds he finds his match. How quickly the old turkey discovers the hawk, a mere speck against the sky, and how quickly the hawk discovers you if you happen to be secreted in the bushes, or behind the fence near which he alights! One advantage the bird surely has, and that is, owing to the form, structure, and position of the eye, it has a much larger field of vision—indeed, can probably see in nearly every direction at the same instant, behind as well as before. Man's field of vision embraces less than half a circle horizontally, and still less vertically; his brow and brain prevent him from seeing within many degrees of the zenith without a movement of the head; the bird, on the other hand, takes in nearly the whole sphere at a glance.

I find I see, almost without effort, nearly every bird within sight in the field or wood I pass through (a flit of the wing, a flirt of the tail are enough, though the flickering leaves do all conspire to hide them), and that with like ease the birds see me, though, unquestionably, the chances are immensely in their favor. The eye sees what it has the means of seeing, truly. You must have the bird in your heart before you find it in the bush.

Locust and Wild Honey

The life of the birds, especially of our migratory songbirds, is a series of adventures and of hair-breadth escapes by flood and field. Very few of them probably die a natural death, or even live out half their appointed days. The home instinct is strong in birds as it is in most creatures; and I am convinced that every spring a large number of those which have survived the Southern campaign return to their old haunts to breed. A Connecticut farmer took me out under his porch, one April day, and showed me a phoebe bird's nest six stories high. The same bird had no doubt returned year after year; and as there was room for only one nest upon her favorite shelf, she had each season reared a new superstructure upon the old as a foundation. I have heard of a white robin—an albino—that nested several years in succession in the suburbs of a

Maryland city. A sparrow with a very marked peculiarity of song I have heard several seasons in my own locality. But the birds do not all live to return to their old haunts; the bobolinks and starlings run a gauntlet of fire from the Hudson to the Savannah, and the robins and meadowlarks and other songbirds are shot by boys and pot-hunters in great numbers—to say nothing of their danger from hawks and owls. But of those that do return, what perils beset their nests, even in the most favored localities! The cabins of the early settlers, when the country was swarming with hostile Indians, were not surrounded by such dangers. The tender households of the birds are not only exposed to hostile Indians in the shape of cats and collectors, but to numerous murderous and bloodthirsty animals, against whom they have no defense but concealment. They lead the darkest kind of pioneer life, even in our gardens and orchards, and under the walls of our houses. Not a day or a night passes, from the time the eggs are laid till the young are flown, when the chances are not greatly in favor of the nest being rifled and its contents devoured—by owls, skunks, minks, and coons at night, and by crows, jays, squirrels, weasels, snakes, and rats during the days. Infancy, we say, is hedged about by many perils; but the infancy of birds is cradled and pillowed in peril.

Signs and Seasons

It usually happens, when the male of any species is killed during the breeding season, that the female soon procures another mate. There are, most likely, always a few unmated birds of both sexes within a given range, and through these the broken links may be restored. Audubon or Wilson, I forget which, tells of a pair of fish hawks, or ospreys, that built their nest in an ancient oak. The male was so zealous in the defense of the young that

The male scarlet tanager's black wings (above) provide a
dramatic contrast to its scarlet feathers. The nest of the Traill's flycatcher
(opposite) is a coarse structure of weed stems and grasses.

he actually attacked with beak and claw a person who attempted to climb into his nest, putting his face and eyes in great jeopardy. Arming himself with a heavy club, the climber felled the gallant bird to the ground and killed him. In the course of a few days the female had procured another mate. But naturally enough the stepfather showed none of the spirit and pluck in defense of the brood that had been displayed by the original parent. When danger was nigh he was seen afar off, sailing around in placid unconcern.

Far and Near

On the whole, there seems to be a system of Women's Rights prevailing among the birds, which, contemplated from the standpoint of the male, is quite admirable. In almost all cases of joint interest, the female bird is the most active. She determines the site of the nest, and is usually the most absorbed in its construction. Generally, she is more vigilant in caring for the young, and manifests the most concern when danger threatens. Hour after hour I have seen the mother of a brood of blue grosbeaks pass from the nearest meadow to the tree that held her nest, with a cricket or grasshopper in her bill, while her better-dressed half was singing serenely on a distant tree or pursuing his pleasure amid the branches.

Yet among the majority of our songbirds the male is most conspicuous both by his color and manners and by his song, and is to that extent a shield to the female. It is thought that the female is humbler clad for her better concealment during incubation. But this is not satisfactory, as in some cases she is relieved from time to time by the male. In the case of the domestic dove, for instance, promptly at midday the cock is found upon the nest. I should say that the dull or neutral tints of the female were a provision of nature for her greater safety at all times, as her life is far more precious in the species than that of the male.

Wake-Robin

The birds do indeed begin with the day. The farmer who is in the field at work while he can yet see stars catches their first matin hymns. In the longest June days the robin strikes up about half past three o'clock, and is quickly followed by the song sparrow, the oriole, the catbird, the wren, the wood thrush, and all the rest of the tuneful choir. Along the Potomac I have heard the Virginia cardinal whistle so loudly and persistently in the treetops above, that sleeping after four o'clock was out of the question. Just before the sun is up, there is a marked lull, during which, I imagine, the birds are at breakfast. While building their nest, it is very early in the morning that they put in their big strokes; the back of their day's work is broken before you have begun yours.

Pepacton

One evening, while seated upon my porch, I had convincing proof that musical or song contests do take place among the birds. Two wood thrushes who had nests nearby sat on the top of a dead tree and pitted themselves against each other in song for over half an hour, contending like champions in a game, and certainly affording the rarest treat in wood thrush melody I had ever had. They sang and sang with unwearied spirit and persistence, now and then changing position or facing in another direction, but keeping within a few feet of each other. The rivalry became so obvious and was so interesting that I finally made it a point not to take my eyes from the singers. The twilight deepened till their forms began to grow dim; then one of the birds could stand the strain no longer, the limit of fair competition had been reached, and seeming to say, "I will silence you, anyhow," it made a spiteful dive at its rival, and in hot pursuit the two disappeared in the bushes beneath the tree. Of course I would not say that the birds were consciously striving to outdo each other in song; it was the old feud between males in the love season, not a war of words or of blows, but of song. Had the birds been birds of brilliant plumage, the rivalry would probably have taken the form of strutting and showing off their bright colors and ornaments.

Ways of Nature

It is a curious habit the wood thrush has of starting its nest with a fragment of newspaper or other paper. Except in remote woods, I think it nearly always puts a piece of paper in the foundation of its nest. Last spring I chanced to be sitting near a tree in which a wood thrush had concluded to build. She came with a piece of paper nearly as large as my hand, placed it upon the branch, stood upon it a moment, and then flew down to the ground. A little puff of wind caused the paper to leave the branch a moment afterward. The thrush watched it eddy slowly down to the ground, when she seized it and carried it back. She placed it in position as before, stood upon it again for a moment, and then flew away. Again the paper left the branch, and sailed away slowly to the ground. The bird seized it again, jerking it about rather spitefully, I thought; she turned it around two or three times, then labored back to the branch with it, upon which she shifted it about as if to hit upon some position in which it would lie more securely. This time she sat down upon it for a moment, and then went away, doubtless with the thought in her head that she would bring something to hold it down. The perverse paper followed her in a few seconds. She seized it again, and hustled it about more than before. As she rose with it

toward the nest, it in some way impeded her flight, and she was compelled to return to the ground with it. But she kept her temper remarkably well. She turned the paper over and took it up in her beak several times before she was satisfied with her hold, and then carried it back to the branch, where, however, it would not stay. I saw her make six trials of it, when I was called away. I think she finally abandoned the restless fragment, probably a scrap that held some "breezy" piece of writing, for later in the season I examined the nest and found no paper in it.

Riverby

The first year of my cabin life a pair of robins attempted to build a nest upon the round timber that forms the plate under my porch roof. But it was a poor place to build in. It took nearly a week's time and caused the birds a great waste of labor to find this out. The coarse material they brought for the foundation would not bed well upon the rounded surface of the timber, and every vagrant breeze that came along swept it off. My porch was kept littered with twigs and weed stalks for days, till finally the birds abandoned the undertaking. The next season a wiser or more experienced pair made the attempt again, and succeeded. They placed the nest against the rafter where it joins the plate; they used mud from the start to level up with and to hold the first twigs and straws, and had soon completed a firm, shapely structure. When the young were about ready to fly it was interesting to note that there was apparently an older and a younger, as in most families. One bird was more advanced than any of the others. Had the parent birds intentionally stimulated it with extra quantities of food, so as to be able to launch their offspring into the world one at a time? At any rate, one of the birds was ready to leave the nest a day and a half before any of

the others. I happened to be looking at it when the first impulse to get outside the nest seemed to seize it. Its parents were encouraging it with calls and assurances from some rocks a few yards away. It answered their calls in vigorous, strident tones. Then it climbed over the edge of the nest upon the plate, took a few steps forward, then a few more, till it was a yard from the nest and near the end of the timber, and could look off into free space. Its parents apparently shouted, "Come on!" But its courage was not quite equal to the leap; it looked around, and seeing how far it was from home, scampered back to the nest, and climbed into it like a frightened child. It had made its first journey into the world, but the home tie had brought it quickly back. The third time its heart was braver, its wings stronger, and leaping into the air with a shout, it flew easily to some rocks a dozen or more yards away. Each of the young in succession, at intervals of nearly a day, left the nest in this manner. There would be the first journey of a few feet along the plate, the first sudden panic at being so far from home, the rush back, a second and perhaps a third attempt, and then the irrevocable leap into the air, and a clamorous flight to a nearby bush or rock. Young birds never go back when they have once taken flight. The first free flap of the wing severs forever the ties that bind them to home.

Far and Near

Being an observer of the birds, of course every curious incident connected with them fell under my notice. Hence, as we stood about our campfire one afternoon looking out over the lake, I was the only one to see a little commotion in the water, half hidden by the near branches, as of some tiny swimmer struggling to reach the shore. Rushing to its rescue in the canoe, I found a yellow-rumpled warbler, quite exhausted, clinging to a twig that hung down into the water. I brought the drenched and helpless thing to camp, and, putting it into a basket, hung it up to dry. An hour or two afterward I heard it fluttering in its prison, and, cautiously lifting the lid to get a better glimpse of the lucky capture, it darted out and was gone in a twinkling. How came it in the water? That was my wonder, and I can only guess that it was a young bird that had never before flown over a pond of water, and, seeing the clouds and blue sky so perfect down there, thought it was a vast opening or gateway into another summer land, perhaps a short cut to the tropics, and so got itself into trouble.

Locusts and Wild Honey

How alert and vigilant the birds are, even when absorbed in building their nests! In an open space in the woods I see a pair of cedar birds [cedar waxwings] collecting moss from the top of a dead tree. Following the direction in which they fly, I soon discover the nest placed in the fork of a small soft maple, which stands amid a thick growth of wild cherry trees and young beeches. Carefully concealing myself beneath it, without any fear that the workmen will hit me with a chip or let fall a tool, I await the return of the busy pair. Presently I hear the well-known note, and the female sweeps down and settles unsuspectingly into the half-finished structure. Hardly have her wings rested before her eye has penetrated my screen, and with a hurried movement of alarm she darts away. In a moment the male, with a tuft of wool in his beak (for there is a sheep pasture near), joins her, and the two reconnoiter the premises from the surrounding bushes. With their beaks still loaded, they move around with a frightened look, and refuse to approach the nest till I have moved off and lain down behind a log.

Wake-Robin

The bluebird is a home bird, and I am never tired of recurring to him. His coming or reappearance in the spring marks a new chapter in the progress of the season; things are never quite the same after one has heard that note. The past spring the males came about a week in advance of the females. A fine male lingered about my grounds and orchard all the time, apparently waiting the arrival of his mate. He called and warbled every day, as if he felt sure she was within earshot, and could be hurried up. Now he warbled half angrily or upbraidingly, then coaxingly, then cheerily

and confidently, the next moment in a plaintive, faraway manner. He would half open his wings, and twinkle them caressingly, as if beckoning his mate to his heart. One morning she had come, but was shy and reserved. The fond male flew to a knothole in an old apple tree, and coaxed her to his side. I heard a fine confidential warble—the old, old story. But the female flew to a near tree, and uttered her plaintive, homesick note. The male went and got some dry grass or bark in his beak, and flew again to the hole in the old tree, and promised unremitting devotion, but the other said "nay," and flew away in the distance. When he saw her going, or rather heard her distant note, he dropped his stuff, and cried out in a tone that said plainly enough, "Wait a minute. One word, please," and flew swiftly in pursuit. He won her before long, however, and early in April the pair were established in one of the four or five boxes I had put up for them, but not until they had changed their minds several times. As soon as the first brood had flown, and while they were yet under their parents' care, they began another nest in one of the other boxes, the female, as usual, doing all the work, and the male all the complimenting.

Locusts and Wild Honey

An observer of the birds is attracted by any unusual sound or commotion among them. In May or June, when other birds are most vocal, the jay is a silent bird; he goes sneaking about the orchards and the groves as silent as a pickpocket; he is robbing bird's nests and he is very anxious that nothing should be said about it; but in the fall none so quick and loud to cry "Thief, thief!" as he. One December morning a troop of jays discovered a little screech owl

*"The great bugaboo of the birds is the owl....
He is a veritable ogre to them, and his presence
fills them with consternation and alarm."*

secreted in the hollow trunk of an old apple tree near my house. How they found the owl out is a mystery, since it never ventures forth in the light of day; but they did, and proclaimed the fact with great emphasis. I suspect the bluebirds first told them, for these birds are constantly peeping into holes and crannies, both spring and fall. Some un-suspecting bird had probably entered the cavity prospecting for a place for next year's nest, or else looking out a likely place to pass a cold night, and then had rushed out with im-portant news. A boy who should unwittingly venture into a bear's den when Bruin was at home could not be more astonished and alarmed than a bluebird would be on finding itself in the cavity of a decayed tree with an owl. At any rate the bluebirds joined the jays in calling the attention of all whom it might concern to the fact that a culprit of some sort was hiding from the light of day in the old ap-ple tree. I heard the notes of warning and alarm and approached to within eyeshot. The bluebirds were cautious and hovered about ut-tering their peculiar twittering calls; but the jays were bolder and took turns looking in at the cavity, and deriding the poor, shrinking owl. A jay would alight in the entrance of the hole and flirt and peer and attitudinize, and then fly away crying "Thief, thief, thief!" at the top of his voice.

I climbed up and peered into the opening, and could just descry the owl clinging to the inside of the tree. I reached in and took him out, giving little heed to the threatening snap-ping of his beak. He was as red as a fox and as yellow-eyed as a cat. He made no effort to escape, but planted his claws in my forefinger and clung there with a grip that soon grew un-comfortable. I placed him in the loft of an out-house in hopes of getting better acquainted with him. By day he was a very willing prisoner, scarcely moving at all, even when approached and touched with the hand, but

looking out upon the world with half-closed, sleepy eyes. But at night what a change; how alert, how wild, how active! He was like another bird; he darted about with wide, fear-ful eyes, and regarded me like a cornered cat. I opened the window, and swiftly, but as silent as a shadow, he glided out into the congenial darkness, and perhaps, ere this, has revenged himself upon the sleeping jay or bluebird that first betrayed his hiding place.

Locusts and Wild Honey

The great bugaboo of the birds is the owl. The owl snatches them from off their roosts at night, and gobbles up their eggs and young in

their nests. He is a veritable ogre to them, and his presence fills them with consternation and alarm.

One season, to protect my early cherries, I placed a large stuffed owl amid the branches of the tree. Such a racket as there instantly began about my grounds is not pleasant to think upon! The orioles and robins fairly "shrieked out their affright." The news instantly spread in every direction, and apparently every bird in town came to see that owl in the cherry tree, and every bird took a cherry, so that I lost more fruit than if I had left the owl indoors. With craning necks and horrified looks the birds alighted upon the branches, and between their screams would snatch off a cherry, as if the act was some relief to their outraged feelings.

Signs and Seasons

If one has always built one's nest upon the ground, and if one comes of a race of ground-builders, it is a risky experiment to build in a tree. The conditions are vastly different. One of my near neighbors, a little song sparrow, learned this lesson the past season. She grew ambitious; she departed from the traditions of her race, and placed her nest in a tree. Such a pretty spot she chose, too—the pendent cradle formed by the interlaced sprays of two parallel

branches of a Norway spruce. These branches shoot out almost horizontally; indeed, the lower ones become quite so in spring, and the side shoots with which they are clothed droop down, forming the slopes of miniature ridges; where the slopes of two branches join, a little valley is formed which often looks more stable than it really is. My sparrow selected one of these little valleys about six feet from the ground, and quite near the walls of the house. Here, she has thought, I will build my nest, and pass the heat of June in a miniature Norway. This tree is the fir-clad mountain, and this little vale on its side I select for my own. She carried up a great quantity of coarse grass and straws for the foundation, just as she would have done upon the ground. On the top of this mass there gradually came into shape the delicate structure of her nest, compacting and refining till its delicate carpet of hairs and threads was reached. So sly as the little bird was about it, too—every moment on her guard lest you discover her secret! Five eggs were laid, and incubation was far advanced, when

the storms and winds came. The cradle indeed did rock. The boughs did not break, but they swayed and separated as you would part your two interlocked hands. The ground of the little valley fairly gave way, the nest tilted over till its contents fell into the chasm. It was like an earthquake that destroys a hamlet.

No born tree-builder would have placed its nest in such a situation. Birds that build at the end of the branch, like the oriole, tie the nest fast; others, like the robin, build against the main trunk; still others build securely in the fork. The sparrow, in her ignorance, rested her house upon the spray of two branches, and when the tempest came the branches parted company and the nest was engulfed.

Riverby

One June day, I found the nest of the yellow-winged sparrow—the sparrow one often hears in our fields and meadows, that has a song that suggests a grasshopper. I was sitting on the fence that bounded a hill meadow, watching the horned larks, and hoping that one of them would disclose the locality of its nest. A few yards from me was a small bush, from the top of which a yellow-winged sparrow was sending out its feeble, stridulous song. Presently a little brown bird came out of the meadow and alighted in the grass but a few yards from the singer. Instantly he flew to the spot, and I knew it was his mate. They seemed to have some conversation together there in the grass, when, in a moment or two, they separated, the male flitting to his perch on the bush and continuing his song, while the female disappeared quickly into the grass ten or more yards away. "The nest is there," I said, "and I must find it." So I walked straight to the spot where the bird had vanished and scrutinized the ground closely. Not seeing the object of my search, I dropped my handkerchief upon the grass, and began walking cautiously about it in circles, covering more and more ground, and scanning closely every foot of the meadow-bottom. Suddenly, when I was four or five yards from my handkerchief, a little dark-brown bird fluttered out almost from under my feet, and the pretty secret was mine.

The nest, made of dry grass and a few hairs, was sunk into the ground—into the great, brownish-gray, undistinguished meadow surface—and held four speckled eggs. The mother bird fluttered through the grass, and tried, by feigning disablement, to lure me away from the spot. I had noticed that the male had ceased singing as soon as I began my search, and had showed much uneasiness. He now joined the female, and two more agitated birds I had never seen. The actions of this bird are quick and nervous at all times; now they became almost frenzied. But I quickly withdrew, and concealed myself behind the fence. After a brief consultation the birds withdrew also, and it was nearly a half-hour before they returned. Then the mother bird, after much feigning and flitting nervously about, dropped into the grass several yards from the nest. I fancied her approaching it in a cautious, circuitous, indirect way.

In the afternoon I came again; also the next day; but at no time did I find the male in song on his old perch. He seemed to take the blame of the accident upon himself; he had betrayed the locality of the nest; and now I found him upon the fence or upon an apple tree far off, where his presence or his song would not give away the precious secret.

The male bird of almost every species is careful about being much in evidence very near the nest. You will generally find him in song along the rim of a large circle of which the nest is the center. I have known poets to represent the bird singing upon its nest, but if this ever happens, it is a very rare occurrence.

Far and Near

Have you heard the song of the field sparrow? If you have lived in a pastoral country with broad upland pastures, you could hardly have missed him. Wilson, I believe, calls him the grass finch, and was evidently unacquainted with his powers of song. The two white lateral quills in his tail, and his habit of running and skulking a few yards in advance of you as you walk through the fields, are sufficient to identify him. Not in meadows or orchards, but in high, breezy pasture grounds, will you look for him. His song is most noticeable after sundown, when other birds are silent; for which reason he has been aptly called the vesper sparrow. The farmer following his team from the field at dusk catches his sweetest strain. His song is not so brisk and varied as that of the song sparrow, being softer and wilder, sweeter and more plaintive. Add the best parts of the lay of the latter to the sweet vibrating chant of the wood sparrow, and you have the evening hymn of the vesper bird—the poet of the plain, unadorned pastures. Go to those broad, smooth, uplying fields where the cattle and sheep are grazing, and sit down in the twilight on one of those warm, clean stones, and listen to this song. On every side, near and remote, from out the short grass which the herds are cropping, the strain rises. Two or three long, silver notes of peace and rest, ending in some subdued trills and quavers, constitute each separate song. Often you will catch only one or two of the bars, the breeze having blown the minor part away. Such unambitious, quiet, unconscious melody! It is one of the most characteristic sounds in nature. The grass, the stones, the stubble, the furrow, the quiet herds, and the warm twilight among the hills, are all subtly expressed in this song; this is what they are at last capable of.

Wake-Robin

August is the month of the high-sailing hawks. The hen-hawk is the most noticeable. He likes the haze and calm of these long, warm days. He is a bird of leisure, and seems always at his ease. How beautiful and majestic are his movements! So self-poised and easy, such an entire absence of haste, such a magnificent amplitude of circles and spirals, such a haughty, imperial grace, and occasionally, such daring aerial evolutions! . . .

The calmness and dignity of this hawk, when attacked by crows or the kingbird, are well worthy of him. He seldom deigns to notice his noisy and furious antagonists, but deliberately wheels about in that aerial spiral, and mounts and mounts till his pursuers grow dizzy and return to earth again.

Wake-Robin

I am sure I would not exchange the quiet surprise and pleasure I feel, as, on rounding some point or curve in the stream, two or more ducks spring suddenly out from some little cove or indentation in the shore, and with an alarum *quack, quack*, launch into the air and quickly gain the free spaces above the treetops, for the satisfaction of the gunner who sees their dead bodies fall before his murderous fire. He has only a dead duck, which, the chances are, he will not find very toothsome at this season, while I have a live duck with whistling wings cleaving the air northward, where, in some lake or river of Maine or Canada, in late summer, I may meet him again with his brood. It is so easy, too, to bag the game with your eye, while your gun may leave you only a feather or two floating upon the water. The duck has wit, and its wit is as quick as, or quicker than, the sportsman's gun. One day in spring I saw a gunner cut down a duck when it had gained an altitude of thirty or forty feet above the stream. At the report it stopped suddenly, turned a somersault, and fell with a splash into the water. It fell like a brick, and disappeared like one; only a feather and a few bubbles marked the spot where it struck. Had it sunk? No; it had dived. It was probably winged, and in the moment it occupied in falling to the water it had decided what to do. It would go beneath the hunter, since it could not escape above him; it could fly in the water with only one wing, with its feet to aid it. The gunner instantly set up a diligent search in all directions, up and down along the shores, peering long and intently into the depths, thrusting his oar into the weeds and driftwood at the edge of the water, but no duck or sign of duck could he find. It was as if the wounded bird had taken to the mimic heaven that looked so sunny and real down there, and gone on to Canada by that route. What astonished me was that the duck should have kept its presence of mind under such trying circumstances, and not have lost a fraction of a second of time in deciding on a course of action. The duck, I am convinced, has more sagacity than any other of our commoner fowl.

Far and Near

The crow has fine manners. He always has the walk and air of a lord of the soil. One morning I put out some fresh meat upon the snow near my study window. Presently a crow came and carried it off, and alighted with it upon the ground in the vineyard. While he was eating of it, another crow came, and, alighting a few yards away, slowly walked up to within a few feet of this fellow and stopped. I expected to see a struggle over the food, as would have been the case with domestic fowls or animals. Nothing of the kind. The feeding crow stopped eating, regarded the other for a moment, made a gesture or two, and flew away. Then the second crow went up to the food, and proceeded to take his share. Presently the first crow came back, when each seized a portion of the food and flew away with it. Their mutual respect and goodwill seemed perfect. Whether it really was so in our human sense, or whether it was simply an illustration of the instinct of mutual support which seems to prevail among gregarious birds, I know not. Birds that are solitary in their habits, like hawks or woodpeckers, behave quite differently toward each other in the presence of their food.

The lives of the wild creatures revolve about two facts or emotions, appetite and fear. Their keenness in discovering food and in discover-

A wingèd gem amid the trees,
A cheery strain upon the breeze
  From treetop sifting down;
A leafy nest in covert low,
When daisies come and brambles blow,
  A mate in Quaker brown.

But most I prize, past summer's prime,
When other throats have ceased to chime,
  Thy faithful treetop strain;
No brilliant bursts our ears enthrall—
A prelude with a "dying fall"
  That soothes the summer's pain.

Where blackcaps sweeten in the shade,
And clematis a bower hath made,
  Or in the bushy fields,
On breezy slopes where cattle graze,
At noon on dreamy August days,
  Thy strain its solace yields.

Oh, bird inured to sun and heat,
And steeped in summer languor sweet,
  The tranquil days are thine.
The season's fret and urge are o'er,
Its tide is loitering on the shore;
  Make thy contentment mine!

Bird and Bough

When the river is at its wildest, usually in March, the eagles appear. They prowl about amid the ice floes, alighting upon them or flying heavily above them in quest of fish, or a wounded duck or other game.

I have counted ten of these noble birds at one time, some seated grim and motionless upon cakes of ice—usually surrounded by crows—others flapping along, sharply scrutinizing the surface beneath. Where the eagles are, there the crows do congregate. The crow follows the eagle, as the jackal follows the lion, in hope of getting the leavings of the royal table. Then I suspect the crow is a real hero-worshiper. I have seen a dozen or more of them sitting in a circle about an eagle upon the ice, all with their faces turned toward him, and apparently in silent admiration of the dusky king.

The eagle seldom or never turns his back upon a storm. I think he loves to face the wildest elemental commotion. I shall long carry the picture of one I saw floating northward on a large raft of ice one day, in the face of a furious gale of snow. He stood with his talons buried in the ice, his head straight out before him, his closed wings showing their strong elbows—a type of stern defiance and power.

This great metropolitan river, as it were, with its floating palaces, and shores lined with villas, is thus an inlet and a highway of the wild and the savage. The wild ducks and geese still follow it north in spring, and south in fall. The loon pauses in his migrations and disports himself in its waters. Seals and otters are occasionally seen in it.

Signs and Seasons

One of the rarest of nests is that of the eagle, because the eagle is one of the rarest of birds. Indeed, so seldom is the eagle seen that its presence always seems accidental. It appears as if merely pausing on the way, while bound for some distant unknown region. . . .

The golden eagle is common to the Northern parts of both hemispheres, and places its eyrie on high precipitous rocks. . . .

The bald eagle, also, builds on high rocks, according to Audubon, though Wilson describes the nest of one which he saw near Great Egg Harbor, in the top of a large yellow pine. It was a vast pile of sticks, sods, sedge, grass, reeds, etc., five or six feet high by four broad, and with little or no concavity. It had

A red-winged blackbird perched on cattails is a familiar spring sight in marshes and along roadside ditches.

been used for many years, and he was told that the eagles made it a sort of home or lodging place in all seasons.

Wake-Robin

Many times during the season I have in my solitude a visit from a bald eagle. There is a dead tree near the summit, where he often perches, and which we call the "old eagle tree." It is a pine, killed years ago by a thunderbolt—the bolt of Jove—and now the bird of Jove hovers about it or sits upon it. I have little doubt that what attracted me to this spot attracts him—the seclusion, the savageness, the elemental grandeur. Sometimes, as I look out of my window early in the morning, I see the eagle upon his perch, preening his plumage, or waiting for the rising sun to gild the mountaintops. When the smoke begins to rise from my chimney, or he sees me going to the spring for water, he concludes it is time for him to be off. But he need not fear the crack of the rifle here; nothing more deadly than field glasses shall be pointed at him while I am around.... What would it profit me could I find and plunder my eagle's nest, or strip his skin from his dead carcass? Should I know him better? I do not want to know him that way. I want rather to feel the inspiration of his presence and noble bearing. I want my interest and sympathy to go with him in his continental voyaging up and down, and in his long, elevated flights to and from his eyrie upon the remote, solitary cliffs. He draws great lines across the sky; he sees the forests like a carpet beneath him, he sees the hills and valleys as folds and wrinkles in a many-colored tapestry; he sees the river as a silver belt connecting remote horizons. We climb mountain peaks to get a glimpse of the spectacle that is hourly spread out beneath him. Dignity, elevation, repose, are his.

Far and Near

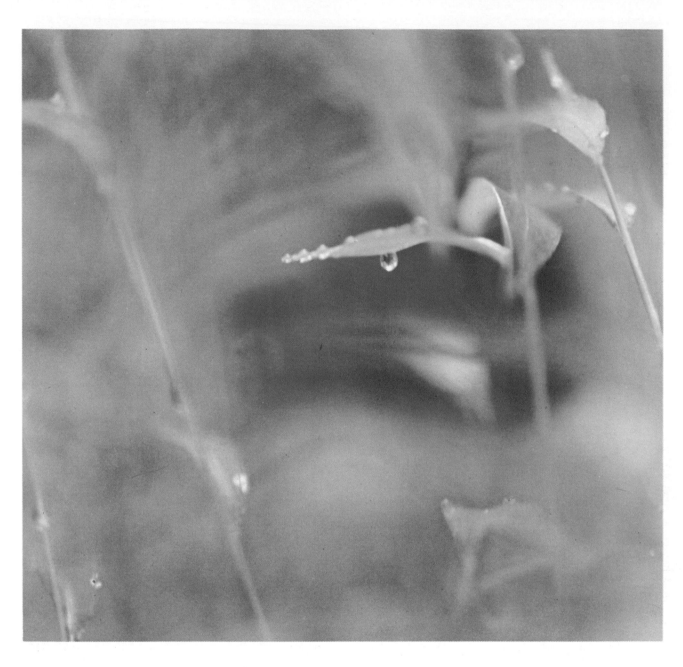

The power to see straight is the rarest of gifts; to see no more and no less than is actually before you; to be able to detach yourself and see the thing as it actually is, uncolored or unmodified by your own sentiments or prepossessions. In short, to see with your reason as well as with your perceptions, that is to be an observer and to read the book of nature aright.

Ways of Nature

One secret of success in observing nature is capacity to take a hint; a hair may show where a lion is hid. One must put this and that together, and value bits and shreds.... How insignificant appear most of the facts which one sees in his walks, in the life of the birds, the flowers, the animals, or in the phases of the landscape, or the look of the sky!—insignificant until they are put through some mental or emotional process and their true value appears. The diamond looks like a pebble until it is cut. One goes to Nature only for hints and half truths. Her facts are crude until you have absorbed them or translated them.

Signs and Seasons

The farmer should be the true naturalist; the book in which it is all written is open before him night and day, and how sweet and wholesome all his knowledge is!

Signs and Seasons

Unadulterated, unsweetened observations are what the real nature lover craves. No man can invent incidents and traits as interesting as the reality.

Ways of Nature

The mind of an observer is like a gun with a hair trigger—it goes at a touch, while the minds of most persons require very vigorous nudging. You must take the hint and take it quickly if you would get up any profitable intimacy with nature. Above all, don't jump to conclusions; look again and again; verify your observations. Be sure the crow is pulling corn, and not probing for grubs, before you kill him. Be sure it is the oriole purloining your grapes, and not the sparrows, before you declare him your enemy. I one day saw hummingbirds apparently probing the ripe yellow cheeks of my finest peaches, but I was not certain till I saw a bird hovering over a particular peach, and then mounting upon a ladder I examined it, when sure enough, the golden cheek was full of pinholes. The orioles destroy many of my earliest pears, but it required much watching to catch them in the very act. I once saw a phoebe bird swoop down upon a raspberry bush and carry a berry to a rail on a near fence, but I did not therefore jump to the conclusion that the phoebe was a berry-eater. What it wanted was the worm in the berry. How do I know? Because I saw it extract something from the berry and fly away.

Riverby

One of my critics has accused me of measuring all things by the standard of my little farm—of thinking that what is not true of animal life there is not true anywhere. Unfortunately my farm *is* small—hardly a score of acres—and its animal life very limited. I have never seen even a porcupine upon it; but I have a hill where one might roll down, should one ever come my way and be in the mood for that kind of play. I have a few possums, a woodchuck or two, an occasional skunk, some red squirrels and rabbits, and many kinds of songbirds. Foxes occasionally cross my acres; and once, at least, I saw a bald eagle devouring a fish in one of my apple trees. Wild ducks, geese, and swans in spring and fall pass across the sky above me. Quail and grouse invade my premises, and of crows I have, at least in bird nesting time, too many.

But I have a few times climbed over my pasture wall and wandered into distant fields. Once upon a time I was a traveler in Asia for the space of two hours—an experience that ought to have yielded me some startling discoveries, but did not. Indeed, the wider I have traveled and observed nature, the more I am convinced that the wild creatures behave just about the same in all parts of the country; that is, under similar conditions. What one observes truly about bird or beast upon his farm of ten acres, he will not have to unlearn, travel as wide or as far as he will. Where the animals are much hunted, they are of course much wilder and more cunning than where they are not hunted. In the Yellowstone National Park we found the elk, deer, and mountain sheep singularly tame; and in the summer, so we were told, the bears board at the big hotels. The wild geese and ducks, too, were tame; and the red-tailed hawk built its nest in a large dead oak that stood quite alone near the side of the road. With us the same hawk hides its nest in a tree in the dense woods, because the farmers unwisely hunt and destroy it. But the cougars and coyotes and bobcats were no tamer in the park than they are in other places where they are hunted.

Indeed, if I had elk and deer and caribou and moose and bears and wildcats and beavers and

otters and porcupines on my farm, I should expect them to behave just as they do in other parts of the country under like conditions: they would be tame and docile if I did not molest them, and wild and fierce if I did. They would do nothing out of character in either case.

Your natural history knowledge of the East will avail you in the West. There is no country, says Emerson, in which they do not wash the pans and spank the babies; and there is no country where a dog is not a dog, or a fox a fox,

or where a hare is ferocious, or a wolf lamblike. The porcupine behaves in the Rockies just as he does in the Catskills; the deer and the moose and the black bear and the beaver of the Pacific slope are almost identical in their habits and traits with those of the Atlantic slope.

Ways of Nature

In a secluded swampy corner of the old Barkpeeling, where I find the great purple orchis in bloom, and where the foot of man or beast seems never to have trod, I linger long, contemplating the wonderful display of lichens and mosses that overrun both the smaller and the larger growths. Every bush and branch and sprig is dressed up in the most rich and fantastic of liveries; and, crowning all, the long bearded moss festoons the branches or sways gracefully from the limbs. Every twig looks a century old, though green leaves tip the end of it. A young yellow birch has a venerable, patriarchal look, and seems ill at ease under such premature honors. A decayed hemlock is draped as if by hands for some solemn festival.

Mounting toward the upland again, I pause reverently as the hush and stillness of twilight come upon the woods. It is the sweetest, ripest hour of the day. And as the hermit's evening hymn goes up from the deep solitude below me, I experience that serene exaltation of sentiment of which music, literature, and religion are but the faint types and symbols.

Wake-Robin

Spring is the inspiration, fall the expiration. Both seasons have their equinoxes, both their filmy, hazy air, their ruddy forest tints, their cold rains, their drenching fogs, their mystic moons; both have the same solar light and warmth, the same rays of the sun; yet, after all, how different the feelings which they inspire! One is the morning, the other the evening; one is youth, the other is age....

It is rarely that an artist succeeds in painting unmistakably the difference between sunrise and sunset; and it is equally a trial of his skill to put upon canvas the difference between early spring and late fall, say between April and November. It was long ago observed that the shadows are more opaque in the morning than in the evening; the struggle between the light and the darkness more marked, the gloom more solid, the contrasts more sharp, etc. The rays of the morning sun chisel out and cut down the shadows in a way those of the setting sun do not. Then the sunlight is whiter and newer in the morning—not so yellow and diffused. A difference akin to this is true of the two seasons I am speaking of. The spring is the morning sunlight, clear and determined; the autumn, the afternoon rays, pensive, lessening, golden.

Winter Sunshine

I pity the person who does not get at least one or two fresh impressions of the charm and sweetness of nature in the spring. Later in the season it gets to be more of an old story; but in March, when the season is early, and in April, when the season is late, there occasionally come days which awaken a new joy in the heart. Every recurring spring one experiences this fresh delight. There is nothing very tangible yet in awakening nature, but there is something in the air, some sentiment in the sunshine and in the look of things, a prophecy of life and renewal, that sends a thrill through the frame. The first sparrow's song, the first robin's call, the first bluebird's warble, the first phoebe's note—who can hear it without emotion? Or the first flock of migrating geese or ducks—how much they bring north with them! When the red-shouldered starlings begin to gurgle in the elms or golden willows along the marshes and watercourses, you will feel spring then; and if you look closely upon the ground beneath them, you will find that sturdy advanced guard of our floral army, the skunk cabbage, thrusting his spear point up through the ooze, and spring will again quicken your pulse.

One seems to get nearer to nature in the early spring days: all screens are removed, the earth everywhere speaks directly to you; she is

not hidden by verdure and foliage; there is a peculiar delight in walking over the brown turf of the fields that one cannot feel later on. How welcome the smell of it, warmed by the sun; the first breath of the reviving earth. How welcome the full, sparkling watercourses, too, everywhere drawing the eye; by and by they will be veiled by the verdure and shrunken by the heat. When March is kind, for how much her slightest favors count! The other evening, as I stood on the slope of a hill in the twilight, I heard a whistling of approaching wings, and presently a woodcock flying low passed near me. I could see his form and his long curved wings dimly against the horizon; his whistling slowly vanished in the gathering night, but his passage made something stir and respond within me. March was on the wing, she was abroad in the soft still twilight searching out the moist, springy places where the worms first come to the surface and where the grass first starts; and her course was up the valley from the south. A day or two later I sat on a hillside in the woods late in the day, amid the pines and hemlocks, and heard the soft, elusive spring call of the little owl—a curious musical undertone hardly separable from the silence; a bell, muffled in feathers, tolling in the twilight of the woods and discernible only to the most alert ear. But it was the voice of spring, the voice of the same impulse that sent the woodcock winging his way through the dusk, that was just beginning to make the pussy willows swell and the grass to freshen in the spring runs.

Occasionally, of a bright, warm, still day in March, such as we have had the present season, the little flying spider is abroad. It is the most delicate of all March tokens, but very suggestive. Its long, waving threads of gossamer, invisible except when the sunlight falls upon them at a particular angle, stream out here and there upon the air, a filament of life, reaching and reaching as if to catch and detain the most subtle of the skyey influences.

Nature is always new in the spring, and lucky are we if it finds us new also.

Riverby

All beginnings in nature afford us a peculiar pleasure. The early spring with its hints and dim prophecies, the first earth odors, the first robin or song sparrow, the first furrow, the first tender skies, the first rainbow, the first wild flower, the dropping bud scales, the awakening voices in the marshes—all these things touch and move us in a way that later developments in the season do not.

Literary Values

become gross, the rays slowly turn brown, and finally wither up and drop. It is a flower no longer, but a receptacle packed with ripening seeds.

A relative of the daisy, the orange-colored hawkweed (*Hieracium aurantiacum*), which within the past twenty years has spread far and wide over New York and New England, is often at the height of its beauty in August, when its deep vivid orange is a delight to the eye. It repeats in our meadows and upon our hilltops the flame of the columbine of May, intensified. The personified August with these flowers in her hair would challenge our admiration and not our criticism. Unlike the daisy, it quickly sprouts again when cut down with the grass in the meadows, and renews its bloom. Parts of New England, at least, have a native August flower quite as brilliant as the hawkweed just described, and far less a usurper; I refer to meadow-beauty, or rhexia, found near the coast, which suggests a purple evening primrose.

Nature has, for the most part, lost her delicate tints in August. She is tanned, hirsute, freckled, like one long exposed to the sun. Her touch is strong and vivid. The coarser, commoner wayside flowers now appear—vervain, eupatorium, mimulus, the various mints, asters, goldenrod, thistles, fireweed, mulleins, motherwort, catnip, blueweed, turtlehead, sunflowers, clematis, evening primrose, lobelia, gerardia, and, in the marshes of the lower Hudson, marshmallows, and vast masses of the purple loosestrife. Mass and intensity take the place of delicacy and furtiveness. The spirit of Nature has grown bold and aggressive; it is rank and coarse; she flaunts her weeds in our faces. She wears a thistle on her bosom. But I must not forget the delicate rose gerardia, which she also wears upon her bosom, and which suggests that, before the season closes,

One of our well-known poets, in personifying August, represents her as coming with daisies in her hair. But an August daisy is a sorry affair; it is little more than an empty, or partly empty, seed vessel. In the Northern States the daisy is in her girlhood and maidenhood in June; she becomes very matronly early in July—fat, faded, prosaic—and by or before August she is practically defunct. . . .

How positively girlish and taking is the daisy during the first few days of its blooming, while its snow-white rays yet stand straight up and shield its tender center somewhat as a hood shields a girl's face! Presently it becomes a perfect disk and bares its face to the sun; this is the stage of its young womanhood. Then its yellow center—its body—begins to swell and

Nature is getting her hand ready for her delicate spring flora. With me this gerardia lines open paths over dry knolls in the woods, and its little purple bells and smooth, slender leaves form one of the most exquisite tangles of flowers and foliage of the whole summer. It is August matching the color and delicacy of form of the fringed polygala of May. I know a half-wild field bordering a wood, which is red with strawberries in June and pink with gerardia in August.

One may still gather the matchless white pond lily in this month, though this flower is in the height of its glory earlier in the season, except in the northern lakes. . . .

The characteristic odors of August are from fruit—grapes, peaches, apples, pears, melons—and the ripening grain; yes, and the blooming buckwheat. Of all the crop and farm odors this last is the most pronounced and honeyed, rivaling that of the flowering locust of May and of the linden in July.

Far and Near

*Frail daisies stand like sentinels (opposite) in front
of a rustic door. A thistle (above) appears coarse in contrast.
"The spirit of Nature has grown bold and aggressive; it is rand and coarse;
she flaunts her weeds in our faces. She wears a thistle on her bosom."*

The typical spring and summer and autumn days, of all shades and complexions—one cannot afford to miss any of them; and when looked out upon from one's own spot of earth, how much more beautiful and significant they are! Nature comes home to one most when he is at home; the stranger and traveler finds her a stranger and a traveler also. One's own landscape comes in time to be a sort of outlying part of himself; he has sowed himself broadcast upon it, and it reflects his own moods and feelings; he is sensitive to the verge of the horizon: cut those trees, and he bleeds; mar those hills, and he suffers. How has the farmer planted himself in his fields; builded himself into his stone walls, and evoked the sympathy of the hills by his struggle!

Signs and Seasons

He who marvels at the beauty of the world in summer will find equal cause for wonder and admiration in winter. It is true the pomp and the pageantry are swept away, but the essential elements remain—the day and the night, the mountain and the valley, the elemental play and succession and the perpetual presence of the infinite sky. In winter the stars seem to have rekindled their fires, the moon achieves a fuller triumph, and the heavens wear a look of a more exalted simplicity. Summer is more wooing and seductive, more versatile and human, appeals to the affections and the sentiments, and fosters inquiry and the art impulse. Winter is of a more heroic cast, and addresses the intellect. The severe studies and disciplines come easier in winter. One imposes larger tasks upon himself, and is less tolerant of his own weaknesses.

The tendinous part of the mind, so to speak, is more developed in winter; the fleshy, in summer. I should say winter had given the bone and sinew to Literature, summer the tissues and blood.

The simplicity of winter has a deep moral. The return of nature, after such a career of splendor and prodigality, to habits so simple and austere, is not lost either upon the head or the heart. It is the philosopher coming back from the banquet and the wine to a cup of water and a crust of bread.

And then this beautiful masquerade of the elements—the novel disguises our nearest friends put on! Here is another rain and another dew, water that will not flow, nor spill, nor receive the taint of an unclean vessel. And if we see truly, the same old beneficence and willingness to serve lurk beneath all.

Look up at the miracle of the falling snow— the air a dizzy maze of whirling, eddying flakes, noiselessly transforming the world, the exquisite crystals dropping in ditch and gutter, and disguising in the same suit of spotless livery all objects upon which they fall. How novel and fine the first drifts! The old, dilapidated fence is suddenly set off with the most fantastic ruffles, scalloped and fluted after an unheard-of fashion! Looking down a long line of decrepit stone wall, in the trimming of which the wind had fairly run riot, I saw, as for the first time, what a severe yet master artist old Winter is. Ah, a severe artist! How stern the woods look, dark and cold and as rigid against the horizon as iron!

All life and action upon the snow have an added emphasis and significance. Every expression is underscored. Summer has few finer pictures than this winter one of the farmer foddering his cattle from a stack upon the clean snow—the movement, the sharply defined figures, the great green flakes of hay, the long file of patient cows, the advance just arriving and pressing eagerly for the choicest morsels, and the bounty and providence it suggests. Or the chopper in the woods—the prostrate tree, the white new chips scattered about, his easy triumph over the cold, his coat hanging to a limb, and the clear, sharp ring of his axe. The woods are rigid and tense, keyed up by the frost, and resound like a stringed instrument. Or the road-breakers, sallying forth with oxen and sleds in the still, white world, the day after the storm, to restore the lost track and demolish the beleaguering drifts.

All sounds are sharper in winter; the air transmits better. At night I hear more distinctly the steady roar of the North Mountain. In summer it is a sort of complacent purr, as the breezes stroke down its sides; but in winter always the same low, sullen growl.

A severe artist! No longer the canvas and the pigments, but the marble and the chisel. When the nights are calm and the moon full, I go out to gaze upon the wonderful purity of the moonlight and the snow. The air is full of latent fire, and the cold warms me—after a different fashion from that of the kitchen stove. The world lies about me in a "trance of snow." The clouds are pearly and iridescent, and seem the farthest possible remove from the condition of a storm—the ghosts of clouds, the indwelling beauty freed from all dross. I see the hills, bulging with great drifts, lift themselves up cold and white against the sky, the black lines of fences here and there obliterated by the depth of the snow. Presently a fox barks away up next the mountain, and I imagine I can almost see him sitting there, in his furs, upon the illuminated surface, and looking down in my direction. As I listen, one answers him from behind the woods in the valley. What a wild winter sound, wild and weird, up among the ghostly hills! Since the wolf has

ceased to howl upon these mountains, and the panther to scream, there is nothing to be compared with it. So wild! I get up in the middle of the night to hear it. It is refreshing to the ear, and one delights to know that such wild creatures are among us. At this season Nature makes the most of every throb of life that can withstand her severity. How heartily she indorses this fox! In what bold relief stand out the lives of all walkers of the snow! The snow is a great telltale, and blabs as effectually as it obliterates. I go into the woods, and know all that has happened. I cross the fields, and if only a mouse has visited his neighbor, the fact is chronicled.

Winter Sunshine

The country is more of a wilderness, more of a wild solitude, in the winter than in the summer. The wild comes out. The urban, the cultivated, is hidden or negatived. You shall hardly know a good field from a poor, a meadow from a pasture, a park from a forest. Lines and boundaries are disregarded; gates and barways are unclosed; man lets go his hold upon the earth; title deeds are deep buried beneath the snow; the best-kept grounds relapse to a state of nature; under the pressure of the cold all the wild creatures become outlaws, and roam abroad beyond their usual haunts. The partridge comes to the orchard for buds; the rabbit comes to the garden and lawn; the crows and jays come to the ash heap and corn-crib, the snow buntings to the stack and to the barnyard; the sparrows pilfer from the domestic fowls; the pine grosbeak comes down from the north and shears your maples of their buds; the fox prowls about your premises at night, and the red squirrels find your grain in the barn or steal the butternuts from your attic. In fact, winter, like some great calamity, changes the status of most creatures and sets

them adrift. Winter, like poverty, makes us acquainted with strange bedfellows.

Signs and Seasons

I have frequently been surprised, in late fall and early winter, to see how unequal or irregular was the encroachment of the frost upon the earth. If there is suddenly a great fall in the mercury, the frost lays siege to the soil and effects a lodgment here and there, and extends its conquests gradually. At one place in the field you can easily run your staff through into the soft ground, when a few rods farther on it will be as hard as a rock. A little covering of dry grass or leaves is a great protection. The moist places hold out long and the spring runs never freeze. You find the frost has gone several inches into the plowed ground, but on going to the woods, and poking away the leaves and debris under the hemlocks and cedars, you find there is no frost at all. The Earth freezes her ears and toes and naked places first, and her body last.

Birds and Poets

Why does snow so kill the landscape and blot out our interest in it? Not merely because it is cold, and the symbol of death—for I imagine as many inches of apple blossoms would have about the same effect—but because it expresses nothing. White is a negative; a perfect blank. The eye was made for color, and for the earthy tints, and, when these are denied it, the mind is very apt to sympathize and to suffer also.

Birds and Poets

We are eager for Winter to be gone, since he, too, is fugitive and cannot keep his place. Invisible hands deface his icy statuary; his chisel has lost its cunning. The drifts, so pure and exquisite, are now earth-stained and weather-

worn—the flutes and scallops, and fine, firm lines, all gone; and what was a grace and an ornament to the hills is now a disfiguration. Like worn and unwashed linen appear the remains of that spotless robe with which he clothed the world as his bride.

But he will not abdicate without a struggle. Day after day he rallies his scattered forces, and night after night pitches his white tents on the hills, and would fain regain his lost ground; but the young prince in every encounter prevails. Slowly and reluctantly the gray old hero retreats up the mountain, till finally the south rain comes in earnest, and in a night he is dead.

Winter Sunshine

The evergreens can keep a secret the year round, some one has said. How well they keep the secret of the shedding of their leaves! So well that in the case of the spruces we hardly know when it does occur. In fact, the spruces do not properly shed their leaves at all, but simply outgrow them, after carrying them an

Opposite: *"The hemlock is a graceful and noble tree."*
Fireweed provides a colorful addition to the dense cover
of hemlocks on a mist-enshrouded hill.

indefinite time. Some of the species carry their leaves five or six years. The hemlock drops its leaves very irregularly: the winds and the storms whip them off; in winter the snow beneath them is often covered with them.

But the pine sheds its leaves periodically, though always as it were stealthily and under cover of the newer foliage. The white pine usually sheds its leaves in midsummer, though I have known all the pines to delay till October. It is on with the new love before it is off with the old. From May till near autumn it carries two crops of leaves, last year's and the present year's. Emerson's inquiry,

How the sacred pine tree adds

To her old leaves new myriads, ...

is framed in strict accordance with the facts. It is to her *old* leaves that she adds the new. Only the new growth, the outermost leaves, are carried over till the next season, thus keeping the tree always clothed and green. As its moulting season approaches, these old leaves, all the rear ranks on the limbs, begin to turn yellow, and a careless observer might think the tree was struck with death, but it is not. The decay stops just where the growth of the previous spring began, and presently the tree stands green and vigorous, with a newly laid carpet of fallen leaves beneath it. . . .

The pine is the tree of silence. Who was the Goddess of Silence! Look for her altars amid the pines—silence above, silence below. Pass from deciduous woods into pine woods of a windy day, and you think the day has suddenly become calm. Then how silent to the foot! One walks over a carpet of pine needles almost as noiselessly as over the carpets of our dwellings. Do these halls lead to the chambers of the great, that all noise should be banished from them? Let the designers come here and get the true pattern for a carpet—a soft yellowish brown with only a red leaf, or a bit of gray

moss, or a dusky lichen scattered here and there; a background that does not weary or bewilder the eye, or insult the ground-loving foot.

How friendly the pine tree is to man—so docile and available as timber, and so warm and protective as shelter! Its balsam is salve to his wounds, its fragrance is long life to his nostrils; an abiding, perennial tree, tempering the climate, cool as murmuring waters in summer and like a wrapping of fur in winter. . . .

In the absence of the pine, the hemlock is a graceful and noble tree. In primitive woods it shoots up in the same manner, drawing the ladder up after it, and attains an altitude of nearly or quite a hundred feet. It is the poor man's pine, and destined to humbler uses than its lordlier brother. It follows the pine like a servitor, keeping on higher and more rocky ground, and going up the minor branch valleys when the pine follows only the main or mother stream. As an ornamental tree it is very pleasing, and deserves to be cultivated more than it is. It is a great favorite with the sylvan folk, too. The ruffed grouse prefer it to the pine; it is better shelter in winter, and its buds are edible. The red squirrel has found out the seeds in its cones, and they are an important part of his winter stores. Some of the rarer warblers, too, like the Blackburnian and the blue yellow-back, I never find except among the hemlocks. . . .

Both the pine and the hemlock make friends with the birch, the maple, and the oak, and one of the most pleasing and striking features of our autumnal scenery is a mountainside sown broadcast with these intermingled trees, forming a combination of colors like the richest tapestry, the dark green giving body and permanence, the orange and yellow giving light and brilliancy.

Signs and Seasons

A turtle defiantly pokes its head out of its shell. Burroughs delighted in observing the habits of these fascinating creatures.

The first chipmunk in March is as sure a token of the spring as the first bluebird or the first robin; and it is quite as welcome. Some genial influence has found him out there in his burrow, deep under the ground, and waked him up, and enticed him forth into the light of day. The red squirrel has been more or less active all winter; his track has dotted the surface of every new-fallen snow throughout the season. But the chipmunk retired from view early in December, and has passed the rigorous months in his nest, beside his hoard of nuts, some feet underground, and hence, when he emerges in March, and is seen upon his little journeys along the fences, or perched upon a log or rock near his hole in the woods, it is another sign that spring is at hand. His store of nuts may or may not be all consumed; it is certain that he is no sluggard, to sleep away these first bright warm days.

Before the first crocus is out of the ground, you may look for the first chipmunk. When I hear the little downy woodpecker begin his spring drumming, then I know the chipmunk is due. He cannot sleep after that challenge of the woodpecker reaches his ear.

Apparently the first thing he does on coming forth, as soon as he is sure of himself, is to go courting. So far as I have observed, the love-making of the chipmunk occurs in March. A single female will attract all the males in the vicinity. One early March day I was at work for several hours near a stone fence, where a female had apparently taken up her quarters. What a train of suitors she had that day! how they hurried up and down, often giving each other a spiteful slap or bite as they passed. The young are born in May, four or five at a birth.

The chipmunk is quite a solitary creature; I have never known more than one to occupy the same den. Apparently no two can agree to live together. What a clean, pert, dapper, nervous little fellow he is! How fast his heart beats, as he stands up on the wall by the roadside, and, with hands spread out upon his breast, regards you intently! A movement of your arm, and he darts into the wall with a saucy *chip-r-r*, which has the effect of slamming the door behind him.

On some still day in autumn, the nutty days, the woods will often be pervaded by an undertone of sound, produced by their multitudinous clucking, as they sit near their dens. It is one of the characteristic sounds of fall.

The chipmunk has many enemies, such as cats, weasels, black snakes, hawks, and owls. One season one had his den in the side of the bank near my study. As I stood regarding his goings and comings, one October morning, I saw him, when a few yards away from his hole, turn and retreat with all speed. As he darted beneath the sod, a shrike swooped down and hovered a moment on the wing just over the hole where he had disappeared. I doubt if the shrike could have killed him, but it certainly gave him a good fright.

It was amusing to watch this chipmunk carry nuts and other food into his den. He had made a well-defined path from his door out through the weeds and dry leaves into the territory where his feeding ground lay. The path was a crooked one; it dipped under weeds, under some large, loosely piled stones, under a pile of chestnut posts, and then followed the remains of an old wall. Going and coming, his motions were like clockwork. He always went by spurts and sudden sallies. He was never for one moment off his guard.

Riverby

Eternal vigilance is the price of life with most of the wild creatures. There is only one among them whose wildness I cannot understand, and that is the common water turtle. Why is this creature so fearful? What are its enemies? I know of nothing that preys upon it. Yet see how watchful and suspicious these turtles are as they sun themselves upon a log or a rock. Before you are fairly in gunshot of them, they slide down into the water and are gone.

The land turtle, or terrapin, on the other hand, shows scarcely a trace of fear. He will indeed pause in his walk when you are very near him, but he will not retreat into his shell till you have poked him with your foot or your cane. He appears to have no enemies; but the little spotted water turtle is as shy as if he were the delicate tidbit that every creature was searching for. I did once find one which a fox had dug out of the mud in winter, and carried a few rods and dropped on the snow, as if he had found he had no use for it.

One can understand the fearlessness of the skunk. Nearly every creature but the farm dog yields to him the right of way. All dread his terrible weapon. If you meet one in your walk in the twilight fields, the chances are that you will turn out for him, not he for you. He may even pursue you, just for the fun of seeing you run. He comes waltzing toward you, apparently in the most hilarious spirits.

The coon is probably the most courageous creature among our familiar wild animals. Who ever saw a coon show the white feather? He will face any odds with perfect composure. I have seen a coon upon the ground, beset by four men and two dogs, and never for a moment losing his presence of mind, or showing a sign of fear. The raccoon is clear grit.

The fox is a very wild and suspicious creature, but curiously enough, when you suddenly come face to face with him, when he is held by a trap, or driven by the hound, his expression is not that of fear, but of shame and guilt. He seems to diminish in size and to be overwhelmed with humiliation. Does he know

himself to be an old thief, and is that the reason of his embarrassment? The fox has no enemies but man, and when he is fairly outwitted, he looks the shame he evidently feels.

In the heart of the rabbit fear constantly abides. How her eyes protrude! She can see back and front and on all sides as well as a bird. The fox is after her, the owls are after her, the gunners are after her, and she has no defense but her speed. She always keeps well to cover. The northern hare keeps in the thickest brush. If the hare or rabbit crosses a broad open exposure it does so hurriedly, like a mouse when it crosses the road. The mouse is in danger of being pounced upon by a hawk, and the hare or rabbit by the snowy owl, or else the great horned owl.

Riverby

As animals get along very well without hands and tools, so they get along very well without reason. Nature has given them tools in their organization in a sense that she has not given them to man—special appliances developed to meet special needs, such as hooks, spears, saws, files, chisels, barbs, drills, shears, probes, stings, drums, fiddles, cymbals, harps, glues, pastes, armors, stilts, pouches, all related to some need of the creature's life; and in the same way she has given them the quality of reason in their instincts. She has given the beaver knives and chisels in his teeth, she has given the woodpeckers drills in their beaks, she has given the leaf-cutters shears in their mandibles, she has given the bees baskets on their hips, she has given stilts to the waders and bills that are spears, to birds of prey claws that are hooks, and to various creatures weapons of offense and defense that man cannot boast of. Man has no tools or ornamental appendages in his organization, but he has that which can make and use these things—arms and hands, and reason to back them up. I can crack my nut with a stone or hammer, but the squirrel has teeth that help him to the kernel. Each of us is armed as best suits his needs. The mink and the otter can take their fish in the water, but I have to have a net, or a hook, or a weapon of some kind when I catch fish. The woodpecker can chisel out a hole in a tree for his nest or his house, with only the weapon nature gave him, but he cannot make a door to it, or patch it if it becomes leaky. The trap-door spider can build a door to her den, because this instinct is one of her special equipments, and is necessary to her well-being. To the woodpecker such a door is not a necessity.

There are but few things we could teach the animals in their own proper sphere. We could give them hints when they are confronted by new problems, as in the case of the beaver above referred to, but in the ordinary course of nature these new problems rarely turn up. We

could teach the beaver a little more system in the use of his material, but this would be of slight value to him; his dam, made very much as a flood makes a dam of driftwood and mud, answers his purpose. Could we teach the birds where to find a milder clime, or the dog how to find his way home, or the horse how to find water in the desert, or the muskrat or the beaver how to plan and construct houses better suited to their purposes? Could we teach the birds how better to hide their nests? Do the conies amid the rocks, that cure their hay before storing it up for winter use, need to take counsel of us? or the timid hare that sleeps with its eyes open, or the sluggish turtle that covers her eggs in the warm sand? Can we instruct the honeybee in her own arts, or the ant in hers? The spider does not need to learn of us how to weave a net, nor the leaf-rolling insect to be taught the use of stitches. I do not know that we first learned the art of papermaking from the hornets, but certain it is that they hold the original patent for making paper from wood pulp; and the little spiders navigated the air before the first balloon was made, and the *Physalia* hoisted her sail long before the first seaman spread his, and the ant-lion dug his pit and the carpenter bee bored his hole long before man had learned these arts. Indeed, many of the arts and crafts of man exist or are foreshadowed in the world of life below him. There is no tool user among the lower animals that I know of, unless we regard one of the solitary wasps as such when she uses a pebble with which to pack down the earth over her den; but there are many curious devices and makeshifts of one kind and another among both plants and animals for defense, for hiding, for scattering of seeds, for cross-fertilization, etc. The wild creatures have all been to school to an old and wise teacher, Dame Nature, who has been keeping

school now, as near as we can calculate, for several million years. And she is not an indulgent teacher, though a very patient one. Her rod is tooth and claw and hunger and cold and drought and flood, and her penalty is usually death. Her ways are not all ways of pleasantness, nor are all her paths paths of peace.

Leaf and Tendril

I have been a seeker of trout from my boyhood, and on all the expeditions in which this fish has been the ostensible purpose I have brought home more game than my creel showed. In fact, in my mature years I find I got more of nature into me, more of the woods, the wild, nearer to bird and beast, while threading my native streams for trout, than in almost any other way. It furnished a good excuse to go forth; it pitched one in the right key; it sent one through the fat and marrowy places of field and wood. Then the fisherman has a harmless, preoccupied look; he is a kind of vagrant that nothing fears. He blends himself with the trees and the shadows. All his approaches are gentle and indirect. He times himself to the meandering, soliloquizing stream; its impulse bears him along. At the foot of the waterfall he sits sequestered and hidden in its volume of sound. The birds know he has no designs upon them, and the animals see that his mind is in the creek. His enthusiasm anneals him, and makes him pliable to the scenes and influences he moves among.

Then what acquaintance he makes with the stream! He addresses himself to it as a lover to his mistress; he wooes it and stays with it till he knows its most hidden secrets. It runs through his thoughts not less than through its banks there; he feels the fret and thrust of every bar and boulder. Where it deepens, his purpose deepens; where it is shallow, he

is indifferent. He knows how to interpret its every glance and dimple; its beauty haunts him for days.

Locusts and Wild Honey

Outside of the [Washington, D.C.] city limits, the great point of interest to the rambler and lover of nature is the Rock Creek region. Rock Creek is a large, rough, rapid stream, which has its source in the interior of Maryland, and flows into the Potomac between Washington and Georgetown. Its course, for five or six miles out of Washington, is marked by great diversity of scenery. Flowing in a deep valley, which now and then becomes a wild gorge with overhanging rocks and high precipitous headlands, for the most part wooded; here reposing in long, dark reaches, there sweeping and hurrying around a sudden

Overleaf: *Splashes of autumn color frame the turbulent cascades of Carrabassett River, Maine.*

One of the tributaries to Rock Creek within this limit is called Piny [Piney] Branch. It is a small, noisy brook, flowing through a valley of great natural beauty and picturesqueness, shaded nearly all the way by woods of oak, chestnut, and beech, and abounding in dark recesses and hidden retreats.

Wake-Robin

One need but pass the boundary of Washington city to be fairly in the country, and ten minutes' walk in the country brings one to real primitive woods. The town has not yet overflowed its limits like the great Northern commercial capitals, and Nature, wild and unkempt, comes up to its very threshold, and even in many places crosses it.

The woods, which I soon reach, are stark and still. The signs of returning life are so faint as to be almost imperceptible, but there is a fresh, earthy smell in the air, as if something had stirred here under the leaves. The crows caw above the wood, or walk about the brown fields. I look at the gray, silent trees long and long, but they show no sign. The catkins of some alders by a little pool have just swelled perceptibly; and, brushing away the dry leaves and debris on a sunny slope, I discover the liverwort just pushing up a fuzzy, tender sprout. But the waters have brought forth. The little frogs are musical. From every marsh and pool goes up their shrill but pleasing chorus. Peering into one of their haunts, a little body of semi-stagnant water, I discover masses of frogs' spawn covering the bottom. I take up great chunks of the cold, quivering jelly in my hands. In some places there are gallons of it. A youth who accompanies me wonders if it would not be good cooked, or if it could not be used as a substitute for eggs. It is a perfect jelly, of a slightly milky tinge, thickly imbedded with black spots about the size of a small

(continued on page 104)

bend or over a rocky bed; receiving at short intervals small runs and spring rivulets, which open up vistas and outlooks to the right and left, of the most charming description—Rock Creek has an abundance of all the elements that make up not only pleasing but wild and rugged scenery. There is, perhaps, not another city in the Union that has on its very threshold so much natural beauty and grandeur, such as men seek for in remote forests and mountains. A few touches of art would convert this whole region, extending from Georgetown to what is known as Crystal Springs, not more than two miles from the present State Department, into a park unequaled by anything in the world. There are passages between these two points as wild and savage, and apparently as remote from civilization, as anything one meets with in the mountain sources of the Hudson or the Delaware.

In the Western Wilderness

John Burroughs appreciated life's special opportunities. He was usually not comfortable in large gatherings, preferring instead to visit and walk with one or two companions. But when larger expeditions gave promise of unlocking more of nature's mysteries, he gladly gave and received his share. To be invited to tour Yellowstone National Park with President Theodore Roosevelt or to visit Alaska with a distinguished party of scientists and naturalists brought him deep satisfaction and expanded his already broad understanding of the workings of nature.

The vast spaces he experienced in the West appealed to him. Glaciers, mountains, ancient rock formations, dense forests filled with waterfalls and shrubs unknown to him, all of these interested him deeply. In 1899, on his Alaskan expedition with John Muir and other dignitaries, he saw new wonders, including one glacier which Muir had explored twenty years previously. He then braved a stormy ocean to go with the party to the tip of Siberia.

In Yellowstone park in 1903 he defended President Roosevelt from an angry correspondent who attacked him for possibly having plans to hunt game. To this charge, Burroughs declared such true sportsmen and nature lovers as Roosevelt should be granted that privilege. It was with quiet glee that he reported Roosevelt's total catch — one mouse — which the President himself skinned and sent to the curator of the Smithsonian Institution to identify the species.

Marked contrasts with his beloved Catskills confronted him everywhere. On the Gustavus Peninsula, Alaska, when the party wanted to get closer to an inland waterfall, they were prevented by an impenetrable forest from reaching their goal. The fallen timber, moss, dense undergrowth and piercing shrubs were so moist that no fire had ever attacked them. They made an effective barrier which the naturalists could not breach, so the waterfall had to be viewed from small boats offshore.

Each day, Burroughs's sharp, intuitive and mellowing eye gathered the observations for his writing. The faces of Indians, appearance of raw, new towns in the Alaskan wilderness, unusual birds, glacial marks on the land, all were absorbed.

Delicate summer leaves color the rugged walls of
Oneonta Creek Gorge in the Columbia River Valley. Burroughs delighted
in witnessing such contrasts in nature on his Western trips.

Alaskan Trip

It was my good fortune during the summer of 1899 to be one of a party of upwards of forty persons whom E. H. Harriman of New York invited to be his guests on a trip to Alaska. The expedition was known as the Harriman Alaska Expedition, and its object was to combine pleasure with scientific research and exploration. The party embraced a number of college professors, several specialists from the biological and geological surveys of the Government at Washington, two or three well-known artists, as many literary men, a mining expert, and several friends and relatives of Mr. Harriman.

We left New York on the afternoon of May 23, in a special train of palace cars, and took ship at Seattle the last day of the month. All west of the Mississippi was new land to me, and there was a good deal of it. Throughout the prairie region, as a farmer, I rejoiced in the endless vistas of beautiful fertile farms, all busy with the spring planting, and reaching from horizon to horizon of our flying train. . . .

A night's run west of Omaha a change comes over the spirit of nature's dream. We have entered upon that sea of vast rolling plains; agriculture is left behind; these gentle slopes and dimpled valleys are innocent of the plow; herds of grazing cattle and horses are seen here and there; now and then a coyote trots away with feigned indifference from the train, looking like a gray, homeless, sheep-killing shepherd dog; at long intervals a low hut or cabin, looking very forlorn; sometimes a wagon track leads away and disappears over the treeless hills. How I wanted to stop the train and run out over those vast grassy billows and touch and taste this unfamiliar nature!

Presently another change comes over the scene: we see the Rockies faint and shadowy in the far distance, their snowclad summits ghostly and dim; the traveler crosses them on the Union Pacific almost before he is aware of it. He expects a nearer view, but does not get it. Their distant snowcapped peaks rise up, or bow down, or ride slowly along the horizon afar off. They seem to elude him; he cannot get near them; they flee away or cautiously work around him. At one point we seemed for hours approaching the Elk Mountains, which stood up sharp and white against the horizon; but a spell was upon us, or upon them, for we circled and circled till we left them behind. . . .

The ride in the train along the south bank of the Columbia toward Portland, past The Dalles, past the Cascades, past Oneonta Gorge and the Multnomah and Latourelle Falls, is a feast of the beautiful and the sublime—the most delicate tints and colors of moss and wild flowers setting off the most rugged alpine scenery. In places the railroad embankment is decked with brilliant patches of red and purple flowers, as if garlanded for a festival. Presently the moss-covered rocks are white-aproned with the clear mountain brooks that cascade down their sides from the dark, mantling pines and cedars above. . . .

The chapters of our sea voyage and Alaskan experiences properly opened on the afternoon of May 30th, when we found our staterooms in our steamer, the *George W. Elder*, received our California contingent, which included John Muir, and made our final preparations for the trip. The steamer was a large iron ship, specially fitted up for our party. Her coal bunkers were full, and she was provisioned for a two months' cruise. We had hunting parties among us that expected to supply us with venison and bear meat, but to be on the safe side we took aboard eleven fat steers, a flock of sheep, chickens and turkeys, a milch cow, and a span of horses. The horses were to be used to transport the hunters and their traps inland

(continued on page 113)

A woods in winter takes on a formidable aspect. These pine trees in the Cascade Mountains stand rigidly on their snowy base.

and to pack out the big game. The hold of our ship looked like a farmer's barnyard....

Dr. Dall was our Alaska specialist, having previously visited the territory thirteen times, and having spent many years there.... In John Muir we had an authority on glaciers, and a thorough one; he looked upon them with the affection and the air of proprietorship with which a shepherd looks upon his flock. The Indians used to call him the Great Ice Chief.

On June 1st, after touching at Victoria, we were fairly launched upon our voyage. Before us was a cruise of several thousand miles, one thousand of which was through probably the finest scenery of the kind in the world that can be viewed from the deck of a ship—the scenery of fiords and mountain-locked bays and arms of the sea. Day after day a panorama unrolls before us with features that might have been gathered from the Highlands of the Hudson, from Lake George, from the Thousand Islands, the Saguenay, and the Rangeley Lakes in Maine, with the addition of towering snowcapped peaks thrown in for a background. The edge of this part of the continent for a thousand miles has been broken into fragments, small and great, as by the stroke of some earth-cracking hammer, and into the openings and channels thus formed the sea flows freely, often at a depth of from one to two thousand feet. It is along these inland ocean highways, through tortuous narrows, up smooth, placid inlets, across broad island-studded gulfs and bays, with now and then the mighty throb of the Pacific felt for an hour or two through some open door in the wall of islands, that our course lay....

For two days Vancouver Island is on our left with hardly a break in its dark spruce forests, covering mountain and vale. On our right is British Columbia, presenting the same endless spruce forests, with peaks of the Coast Range, eight or ten thousand feet high, in the background, and only an occasional sign of human life on shore. . . .

As we progress, many deep ravines are noted in vast recesses in the mountains, scooped out by the old glaciers. They are enormous rocky bowls which we imagine hold crystal lakes; foaming streams pour out of them into the channel. Far up, silver threads of water, born of the melting snows, are seen upon the vast faces of the rocks. Some of them course down the tracks of old landslides; others are seen only as they emerge from dark spruces.

The snow upon the mountaintops looks new-fallen; our glasses bring out the sharp curling edges of the drifts. Here and there along the shore below are seen the rude huts of trappers and hunters. The eternal spruce and hemlock forests grow monotonous. The many dry, white trunks of dead trees, scattered evenly through the forest, make the mountains look as if a shower of gigantic arrows had fallen upon them from the sky. Gulls, loons, and scoters are seen at long intervals.

Snow avalanches have swept innumerable paths, broad and narrow, down through the spruce forest. Those great glacier basins on our left invite inspection, so we send a party ashore to examine one of them. They do not find the expected lake, but in its stead a sphagnum bog, through which the creek winds its way. Fresh tracks and other signs of deer are seen.

In mid-afternoon we turn into Lowe Inlet, a deep, narrow, mountain-locked arm of the sea on our right, with a salmon cannery at the head of it, and a large, rapid trout stream making a fine waterfall. Here, among the employees of the cannery, we see our first Alaskan Indians and note their large, round, stolid, innocent faces. Here also some of us get our first taste of Alaska woods. In trying to make our way to the falls we are soon up to our necks amid moss, fallen timber, and devil's club. Progress is all but impossible, and those who finally reach the falls do so by withdrawing from the woods and taking to boats. Traversing Alaskan forests must be a trying task even to deer and bears. They have apparently never been purged or thinned by fire—too damp for that—and they are choked with the accumulation of ages. Two or three generations of fallen trees cross one another in all directions amid the rocks, with moss over all like a deep fall of snow, and worse still, thickly planted with devil's club. This is a shrub as high as your head, covered with long sharp spines and with large thorny leaves. It is like a blackberry bush with thorns ten times multiplied. It hedges about these mossy cushions as with the fangs of serpents. One can hardly touch it without being stung. The falls are the outlet of a deep, hidden, enticing valley, with a chain of beautiful lakes, we were told, but our time was too brief to explore it. The winter wren was found here, and the raven, and a species of woodpecker.

It is much easier in Alaska to bag a glacier than a bear; hence our glacial party, made up of John Muir, Gilbert, and Palache, who set out to explore the head of Glacier Bay, was more successful than the hunters. They found more glaciers than they were looking for. One large glacier of twenty years ago had now become two, not by increasing but by diminishing; the main trunk had disappeared, leaving the two branches in separate valleys. All the glaciers of this bay, four or five in number, were found to have retreated many hundred feet since Muir's first visit, two decades earlier. . . .

We were in the midst of strange scenes, hard to render in words: the miles upon miles of moraines upon either hand, gray, loosely piled,

(continued on page 118)

*Steep, tree-lined mountains tower above a calm sea inlet
at Granite Mountain, Alaska. Burroughs was awed by the fjords
he saw on his sea voyage up the Inside Passage.*

*Overleaf: Snowcapped peaks and meandering glaciers
dominate this panoramic view of Glacier Bay, Alaska. This area is a
national monument and the largest unit in the National Park System.*

A i
its name,
gray o
fro

was a te
from the

Kadiak
all of u
highest p
were epi
were ce
than any
go back
there to
peaceful
pastoral,
ged; such
such blu
such a v
the west
Bewitchi
freshness

Accord
outward
Seal Isla
wish to
midnight
man, "w
barren sl

The fo
noon, wh
into suns
coast of S
the horiz
on the r
weight o
iquities.
decrepit
streaked
was the
was Plov
we drop
shaped s
shore. O
campmen
soon asti

scooped
to two
water d
ice; the
smoothe
and snov
from bot
pling, sta
terrible
shore to

We sa
we scrai
yesterda
rocks an
the dista
extensiv
within tl
again; w
loaded w
ing mate
tion in tl
dredgers
along the
the low
depressi
scapes—
der of th

On the
Uyak Ba
Kadiak [
prospect
hills and
the eye a

We ha
that afte
scattered
the valle
near a la
scape gar
grade and
grass and
Here we

blue I ever saw in a wild flower. Here also we saw and heard the Lapland longspur and the yellow wagtail. A flock of male eider ducks was seen in the bay....

On the 25th we were at Juneau again, taking coal and water. The only toad I saw in Alaska I saw this day, as it was fumbling along in the weeds by the roadside, just out of Juneau. Here also I gathered my first salmonberries—a kind of raspberry an inch in diameter, with a slightly bitterish flavor, but very good.

The lovely weather still favored us on our return trip down the inland passage....

We had three tons of coal left in our bunkers, but of our little stock farm down below only the milch cow remained. She had been to Siberia and back, and had given milk all the way.

No voyagers were ever more fortunate than we. No storms, no winds, no delays nor accidents to speak of, no illness. We had gone far and fared well.

Far and Near

Southwest and Yosemite

In making the journey to the great Southwest—Colorado, New Mexico, and Arizona—if one does not know his geology, he is pretty sure to wish he did, there is so much geology scattered over all these Southwestern landscapes, crying aloud to be read. The book of earthly revelation, as shown by the great science, lies wide open in that land, as it does in few other places on the globe....

The rocks attracted me more than the birds, the sculpturing of the landscapes engaged my attention more than the improvements of the farms—what Nature had done more than what man was doing. The purely scenic aspects of the country are certainly remarkable, and the human aspects interesting, but underneath these things, and striking through them, lies a vast world of time and change that to me is still more remarkable, and still more interesting....

Opposite: The Grand Canyon inspired Burroughs with its majesty.
"The immensity of the scene, its tranquillity, its order, its strange, new beauty, and
the monumental character of its many forms—all these tend to beget in the
beholder an attitude of silent wonder and solemn admiration...."

As one leaves the prairie states and nears the great Southwest, he finds Nature in a new mood—she is dreaming of cañons [canyons]; both cliffs and soil have cañon stamped upon them, so that your eye, if alert, is slowly prepared for the wonders of rock carving it is to see on the Colorado. The cañon form seems inherent in soil and rock. The channels of the little streams are cañons, vertical sides of adobe soil, as deep as they are broad, rectangle grooves in the ground....

A friend of mine who took a lively interest in my Western trip wrote me that he wished he could have been present with his kodak when we first looked upon the Grand Cañon. Did he think he could have got a picture of our souls? His camera would have shown him only our silent, motionless forms as we stood transfixed by that first view of the stupendous spectacle. Words do not come readily to one's lips, or gestures to one's body, in the presence of such a scene. One of my companions said that the first thing that came into her mind was the old text, "Be still, and know that I am God." To be still on such an occasion is the easiest thing in the world, and to feel the surge of solemn and reverential emotions is equally easy; is, indeed, almost inevitable. The immensity of the scene, its tranquillity, its order, its strange, new beauty, and the monumental character of its many forms—all these tend to beget in the beholder an attitude of silent wonder and solemn admiration....

It is quite worthwhile to go down into the cañon on muleback, if only to fall in love with a mule, and to learn what a surefooted, careful, and docile creature, when he is on his good behavior, a mule can be. My mule was named "Johnny," and there was soon a good understanding between us. I quickly learned to turn the whole problem of that perilous descent over to him. He knew how to take the sharp turns and narrow shelves of that steep zigzag much better than I did. I do not fancy that the thought of my safety was "Johnny's" guiding star; his solicitude struck nearer home than that. There was much ice and snow on the upper part of the trail, and only those slender little legs of "Johnny's" stood between me and a tumble of two or three thousand feet. How cautiously he felt his way with his round little feet, as, with lowered head, he seemed to be scanning the trail critically! Only when he swung around the sharp elbows of the trail did his forefeet come near the edge of the brink. Only once or twice at such times, as we hung for a breath above the terrible incline, did I feel a slight shudder....

It is worthwhile to make the descent in order to look upon the river which has been the chief quarryman in excavating the cañon, and to find how inadequate it looks for the work ascribed to it. Viewed from where we sat, I judged it to be forty or fifty feet broad, but I was assured that it was between two and three hundred feet. Water and sand are ever symbols of instability and inconstancy, but let them work together, and they saw through mountains, and undermine the foundations of the hills.

It is always worthwhile to sit or kneel at the feet of grandeur, to look up into the placid faces of the earth gods and feel their power, and the tourist who goes down into the cañon certainly has this privilege. We did not bring back in our hands, or in our hats, the glory that had lured us from the top, but we seemed to have been nearer its sources, and to have brought back a deepened sense of the magnitude of the forms, and of the depth of the chasm which we had heretofore gazed upon from a distance.

Time and Change

The splendor of Yosemite National Park, California, is evident no matter what the season. Snow covers the entrance to the valley (below) while new spring blossoms (opposite) frame Yosemite Falls.

O

Man
leave
the wo
areas
to sha
the loc
contin

Som
times i
him ov
genial
all lovi
of the
and m
looked
a mello

The
these s
attract

Opposi
While

Going from the Grand Cañon to Yosemite is going from one sublimity to another of a different order. The cañon is the more strange, unearthly, apocryphal, appeals more to the imagination, and is the more overwhelming in its size, its wealth of color, and its multitude of suggestive forms. But for quiet majesty and beauty, with a touch of the sylvan and pastoral, too, Yosemite stands alone. One could live with Yosemite, camp in it, tramp in it, winter and summer in it, and find nature in her tender and human, almost domestic moods, as well as in her grand and austere. But I do not think one could ever feel at home in or near the Grand Cañon; it is too unlike anything we have ever known upon the earth . . . .

[Yosemite's] many waterfalls fluttering like white lace against its vertical granite walls, its smooth, level floor, its noble pines and oaks, its open glades, its sheltering groves, its bright, clear, winding river, its soft voice of many waters, its flowers, its birds, its grass, its verdure, even its orchards of blooming apple trees, all inclosed in this tremendous granite frame—what an unforgettable picture it all makes, what a blending of the sublime and the homelike and familiar it all is! It is the waterfalls that make the granite alive, and bursting into bloom as it were. What a touch they give! how they enliven the scene! What music they evoke from these harps of stone! . . .

Yosemite won my heart at once, as it seems to win the hearts of all who visit it. In my case many things helped to do it, but I am sure a robin, the first I had seen since leaving home, did his part. He struck the right note, he brought the scene home to me, he supplied the link of association. There he was, running over the grass or perching on the fence, or singing from a treetop in the old familiar way. Where the robin is at home, there at home am I . . . .

to hang you with her dangling ropes, or impale you on her thorns, or engulf you in her ranks of gigantic ferns. Her mood is never as placid and sane as in the North. There is a tree in the Hawaiian woods that suggests a tree gone mad. It is called the hau-tree [*Hibiscus tiliaceus*]. It lies down, squirms, and wriggles all over the ground like a wounded snake; it gets up, and then takes to earth again. Now it wants to be a vine, now it wants to be a tree. It throws somersaults, it makes itself into loops and rings, it rolls, it reaches, it doubles upon itself. Altogether it is the craziest vegetable growth I

ever saw. Where you can get it up off the ground and let it perform its antics on a broad skeleton framework, it makes a cover that no sunbeam can penetrate. . . .

We reached the [Haleakala] summit before the sun reached the horizon, and our eyes looked forth upon a strange world, indeed. On one hand the vast sea of cloud, into which the sun was about to drop, rolled away from the mountain below us, with its white surface and the irregular masses rising up from it, suggesting a sea of floating ice. Through rifts in it we caught occasional glimpses of the Pacific—

Opposite: *"On the other hand was the vast crater of Haleakala, . . . in which the shadows were deepening, and which looked like some burned-out Hades."*

blue, vague, mystical gulfs that seemed filled with something less substantial than water. On the other hand was the vast crater of Haleakala, two thousand feet deep, and many miles across, in which the shadows were deepening, and which looked like some burned-out Hades.

We stood or sat on the jagged edge and saw the day depart and the night come down, the glory of cloud and sea and sunset on the one hand, and on the other side the fearful chasm of the extinct volcano, red and black and barren, with the hosts of darkness gathering in it. It was like a seat between heaven and hell. Then later, when the Southern Cross came out and rose above the awful gulf, the scene was most impressive. . . .

I arose about two o'clock, and made my way out into the star-blazing night. Such glory of the heavens I had never before seen. I had never before been lifted up so near them, and hence had never before seen them through so rarefied an atmosphere. The clouds and vapors had disappeared, and all the hosts of heaven were magnified. The Milky Way seemed newly paved and swept. There was no wind and no sound. The mighty crater was a gulf of blackness, but the sky blazed with light.

The dawn comes early on such a mountain-top, and before four o'clock we were out under the fading stars. As we had seen the day pass into night, surrounded by these wonderful scenes, now we saw the night pass into day, and the elemental grandeur on every hand reborn before us. There was not a wisp of cloud or fog below us or about us to blur the great picture. The sun came up from behind the vast, long, high wall of the Pacific that filled the eastern horizon, and the shadows fled from the huge pile of mountain in the west. . . .

After breakfast we still haunted for an hour or more the brink of the great abyss, where one seemed to feel the pulse of primal time, loath to tear ourselves away, loath also to take a last view of the panorama of land and sea, lit by the morning sun, which spread out far below us. To the southeast we could dimly see the outlines of the island of Hawaii, with a faint gleam of snow on its great mountain Mauna Loa, nearly fourteen thousand feet high. . . .

At the Volcano House [on Mauna Loa] they keep a book in which tourists write down their impressions of the volcano. A distinguished statesman had been there a few days before us, and had written a long account of his impressions, closing with this oratorical sentence: "No pen, however gifted, can describe, no brush, however brilliant, can portray the wonders we have been permitted to behold." I could not refrain from writing under it, "I have seen the orthodox hell, and it's the real thing."

That huge kettle of molten metal, mantling and bubbling, how it is impressed upon my memory! It is a vestige of the ancient cosmic fire that once wrapped the whole globe in its embrace. It had a kind of brutal fascination. One could not take one's eyes from it. That network of broad, jagged, fiery lines defining those black, smooth masses, or islands, of floating matter told of a side of nature we had never before seen. We lingered there on the brink of the fearful spectacle till night came on, and the sides of the mighty caldron, and the fog-clouds above it, glowed in the infernal light. Not so white as the metal pouring from a blast furnace, not so hot, a more sullen red, but welling up from the central primordial fires of the earth. This great pot has boiled over many times in the recent past, as the lava beds we traveled over testify, and it will probably boil over again.

Time and Change

Camping in the Wilderness

John Burroughs entered into deep friendships with few people, but those few had his loyal affection and appreciation over the years. When referring to Walt Whitman, from the time their friendship began during the Civil War years in the nation's capital, he often used the word "noble." He frequently recalled Whitman's compassionate conversation with a wounded, lonely soldier on a Washington street during the war. His account of this episode reveals his own shyness, coupled with his longing to communicate intimately with his fellow man.

Nobility filled him with wonder wherever he found it, be it in nature or man. Other friends of renown included Thomas Edison, Henry Ford, John Muir and Theodore Roosevelt. These men, who appreciated Burroughs's great love of nature, were his favored companions on trips into the wilderness.

Burroughs had a calm, accepting attitude towards both good and ill fortune during his camping trips. Multitudes of today's campers protect themselves from nature with streamlined equipment and luxurious provisions. For Burroughs, a century ago, the deepest pleasure came from the untoward, from living for a few days on fresh milk and berries, from seeking temporary shelter in an abandoned building whose roof gave slight protection, or from retracing steps away from an unexpected bear.

Each detail mattered to him. Selecting companions, deciding whether to aim at a distant and new locale or to explore further his Catskills, and choosing the goal for the trip were all given careful thought. It bored him to go outdoors just to look around—there must be a point to it. Seeking wild game, scaling a tricky mountain, fishing for elusive trout were basic purposes upon which he could build a memorable camping trip. Pleasure was not governed by distance; he could enjoy the far away, but he also maintained a lifelong affection for the wilderness areas near his door.

Burroughs's hope was to experience, to feel, to enter into the spirit of each hour, undeterred by insects, rain, cold, shortage of food, even uncertainty about his exact location. In the wilderness, nature was the provider, campers the recipients. Surprises, bounties and problems were delivered in random lots, seasoning each trip and giving it unique value.

The Adirondacks, here along the Ausable River, provided Burroughs with many convenient areas in which he could observe nature and experience the trials and rewards of wilderness camping.

Whom shall one take with him when he goes a-courting Nature? This is always a vital question. There are persons who will stand between you and that which you seek: they obtrude themselves; they monopolize your attention; they blunt your sense of the shy, half-revealed intelligences about you. I want for companion a dog or a boy, or a person who has the virtues of dogs and boys—transparency, good nature, curiosity, open sense, and a nameless quality that is akin to trees and growth and the inarticulate forces of nature. With him you are alone, and yet have company; you are free; you feel no disturbing element; the influences of nature stream through him and around him; he is a good conductor of the subtle fluid. The quality or qualification I refer to belongs to most persons who spend their lives in the open air—to soldiers, hunters, fishers, laborers, and to artists and poets of the right sort.

Pepacton

The Delaware has a way of dividing up that is very embarrassing to the navigator. It is a stream of many minds: its waters cannot long agree to go all in the same channel, and whichever branch I took I was pretty sure to wish I had taken one of the others. I was constantly sticking on rifts, where I would have to dismount, or running full tilt into willow banks, where I would lose my hat or endanger my fishing tackle....

In the woods, things are close to you, and you touch them and seem to interchange something with them; but upon the river, even though it be a narrow and shallow one, you are more isolated, farther removed from the soil and its attractions, and an easier prey to the unsocial demons. The long, unpeopled vistas ahead; the still, dark eddies; the endless monotone and soliloquy of the stream; the unheeding rocks basking like monsters along the shore, half out of the water, half in; a solitary heron starting up here and there, as you rounded some point, and flapping disconsolately ahead till lost to view, or standing like a gaunt specter on the umbrageous side of the mountain, his motionless form revealed against the dark green as you passed; the trees and willows and alders that hemmed you in on either side, and hid the fields and the farmhouses and the road that ran nearby— these things and others ... cast a gloom over my spirits.

Pepacton

Our next move was a tramp of about twelve miles through the [Adirondack] wilderness, most of the way in a drenching rain, to a place called the Lower Iron Works, situated on the road leading in to Long Lake....

On the afternoon of our arrival, and also the next morning, the view was completely shut off by the fog. But about the middle of the forenoon the wind changed, the fog lifted and revealed to us the grandest mountain scenery we had beheld on our journey. There they sat about fifteen miles distant, a group of them— Mount Marcy, Mount McIntyre, and Mount Colden, the real Adirondack monarchs. It was an impressive sight, rendered doubly so by the sudden manner in which it was revealed to us by that scene-shifter the Wind.

I saw blackbirds at this place, and sparrows, and the solitary sandpiper, and the Canada woodpecker, and a large number of hummingbirds. Indeed, I saw more of the latter here than I ever before saw in any one locality. Their squeaking and whirring were almost incessant....

About half a mile northeast of the village is Lake Henderson, a very irregular and picturesque sheet of water, surrounded by dark evergreen forests, and abutted by two or three bold promontories with mottled white and gray rocks. Its greatest extent in any one direction is perhaps less than a mile. Its waters are perfectly clear and abound in lake trout. A considerable stream flows into it which comes down from Indian Pass.

A mile south of the village is Lake Sanford. This is a more open and exposed sheet of water and much larger. From some parts of it Mount Marcy and the gorge of the Indian Pass are seen to excellent advantage. The Indian Pass shows as a huge cleft in the mountain, the gray walls rising on one side perpendicularly for many hundred feet. This lake abounds in white and yellow perch and in pickerel; of the latter single specimens are often caught which weigh fifteen pounds. There were a few wild ducks on both lakes....

The land on the east side of the lake had been burnt over, and was now mostly grown up with wild cherry and red raspberry bushes. Ruffed grouse were found here in great numbers. The Canada grouse was also common.... Wild pigeons were quite numerous also. These latter recall a singular freak of the sharp-shinned hawk. A flock of pigeons alighted on the top of a dead hemlock standing in the edge of a swamp. I got over the fence and moved toward them across an open space. I had not

*A group of white-tailed deer in their natural
setting is a marvelous scene to encounter.*

taken many steps when, on looking up, I saw
the whole flock again in motion flying very
rapidly around the butt of a hill. Just then this
hawk alighted on the same tree. I stepped back
into the road and paused a moment, in doubt
which course to go. At that instant the little
hawk launched into the air and came as
straight as an arrow toward me. I looked in
amazement, but in less than half a minute he
was within fifty feet of my face, coming full
tilt as if he had sighted my nose. Almost in
self-defense I let fly one barrel of my gun, and
the mangled form of the audacious marauder
fell literally between my feet.

Of wild animals, such as bears, panthers,
wolves, wildcats, etc., we neither saw nor
heard any in the Adirondacks. "A howling
wilderness," Thoreau says, "seldom ever
howls. The howling is chiefly done by the
imagination of the traveler." Hunter said he
often saw bear tracks in the snow, but had
never yet met Bruin. Deer are more or less
abundant everywhere, and one old sportsman
declares there is yet a single moose in these
mountains....

But better than fish or game or grand scenery, or any adventure by night or day, is the
wordless intercourse with rude Nature one has
on these expeditions. It is something to press
the pulse of our old mother by mountain lakes
and streams, and know what health and vigor
are in her veins, and how regardless of observation she deports herself.

Wake-Robin

It was after sunset when we turned back,
and before we had got halfway up the mountain it began to be quite dark. We were often
obliged to rest our packs against trees and take
breath, which made our progress slow. Finally
a halt was called, beside an immense flat rock
which had paused in its slide down the moun-

ems," as Thoreau's Indian aptly named the
midges, soon found us out, and after the fire
had gone down annoyed us much.

Wake-Robin

Not the least of the charm of camping out is
your campfire at night. What an artist! What
pictures are boldly thrown or faintly outlined
upon the canvas of the night! Every object,
every attitude of your companion, is striking
and memorable. You see effects and groups
every moment that you would give money to
be able to carry away with you in enduring
form. How the shadows leap, and skulk, and
hover about! Light and darkness are in perpetual tilt and warfare, with first the one
unhorsed, then the other. The friendly and
cheering fire, what acquaintance we make
with it! We had almost forgotten there was
such an element, we had so long known only
its dark offspring, heat. Now we see the wild
beauty uncaged and note its manner and
temper. How surely it creates its own draft and

tain, and we prepared to encamp for the night.
A fire was built, the rock cleared off, a small
ration of bread served out, our accoutrements
hung up out of the way of the hedgehogs that
were supposed to infest the locality, and then
we disposed ourselves for sleep. If the owls or
porcupines (and I think I heard one of the latter in the middle of the night) reconnoitered
our camp, they saw a buffalo robe spread upon
a rock, with three old felt hats arranged on one
side, and three pairs of sorry-looking cowhide
boots protruding from the other.

When we lay down, there was apparently
not a mosquito in the woods; but the "no-see-

*The stillness of the winter woods is a peaceful scene. As
spring approaches, the snow melts first around the trunks of trees
and bushes, providing the moisture needed for opening buds.*

A view from the summit of Mount Jo in the Adirondacks (above) shows a placid Heart Lake and the dense trees that cover Mount Colden (left), Wright Peak (right center) and Algonquin Peak (right background). A glowing campfire (opposite) promotes friendly companionship when camping out.

sets the currents going, as force and enthusiasm always will! It carves itself a chimney out of the fluid and houseless air. A friend, a ministering angel, in subjection; a fiend, a fury, a monster, ready to devour the world, if ungoverned. By day it burrows in the ashes and sleeps; at night it comes forth and sits upon its throne of rude logs, and rules the camp, a sovereign queen. . . .

What does the camper think about when lounging around the fire at night? Not much—of the sport of the day, of the big fish he lost and might have saved, of the distant settlement, of tomorrow's plans. An owl hoots off in the mountain and he thinks of him; if a wolf were to howl or a panther to scream, he would think of him the rest of the night. As it is, things flicker and hover through his mind, and

he hardly knows whether it is the past or the present that possesses him. Certain it is, he feels the hush and solitude of the great forest, and, whether he will or not, all his musings are in some way cast upon that huge background of the night. Unless he is an old camper-out, there will be an undercurrent of dread or half fear. My companion said he could not help but feel all the time that there ought to be a sentinel out there pacing up and down. One seems to require less sleep in the woods, as if the ground and the untempered air rested and refreshed him sooner. The balsam and the hemlock heal his aches very quickly.

Locusts and Wild Honey

We were encamping in the primitive woods, by a little trout lake which the mountain car-

ried high on his hip, like a soldier's canteen. There were wives in the party, curious to know what the lure was that annually drew their husbands to the woods. That magical writing on a trout's back they would fain decipher, little heeding the warning that what is written here is not given to woman to know.

Our only tent or roof was the sheltering arms of the great birches and maples. What was sauce for the gander should be sauce for the goose, too, so the goose insisted.

A luxurious couch of boughs upon springing poles was prepared, and the night should be not less welcome than the day, which had indeed been idyllic. (A trout dinner had been served by a little spring brook, upon an improvised table covered with moss and decked with ferns, with strawberries from a near clearing.)

At twilight there was an ominous rumble behind the mountains. I was on the lake, and could see what was brewing there in the west.

As darkness came on, the rumbling increased, and the mountains and the woods and the still air were such good conductors of sound that the ear was vividly impressed. One seemed to feel the enormous convolutions of the clouds in the deep and jarring tones of the thunder. The coming of night in the woods is alone peculiarly impressive, and it is doubly so when out of the darkness comes such a voice as this. But we fed the fire the more industriously, and piled the logs high, and kept the gathering gloom at bay by as large a circle of light as we could command. The lake was a pool of ink and as still as if congealed; not a movement or a sound, save now and then a

"It was a regular meteorological carnival, and the revelers were drunk with the wild sport. The apparent nearness of the clouds and the electric explosion was something remarkable."

terrific volley from the cloud batteries now fast approaching. By nine o'clock little puffs of wind began to steal through the woods and tease and toy with our fire. Shortly after, an enormous electric bombshell exploded in the treetops over our heads, and the ball was fairly opened. Then followed three hours, with only two brief intermissions, of as lively elemental music and as copious an outpouring of rain as it was ever my lot to witness. It was a regular meteorological carnival, and the revelers were drunk with the wild sport. The apparent nearness of the clouds and the electric explosion was something remarkable. Every discharge seemed to be in the branches immediately overhead and made us involuntarily cower, as if the next moment the great limbs of the trees, or the trees themselves, would come crashing down. The mountain upon which we were encamped appeared to be the focus of three distinct but converging storms. The last two seemed to come into collision immediately over our campfire, and to contend for the right of way, until the heavens were ready to fall and both antagonists were literally spent. We stood in groups about the struggling fire, and when the cannonade became too terrible would withdraw into the cover of the darkness, as if to be a less conspicuous mark for the bolts; or did we fear the fire, with its currents, might attract the lightning? At any rate, some other spot than the one where we happened to be standing seemed desirable when those onsets of the contending elements were the most furious. Something that one could not catch in his hat was liable to drop almost anywhere any minute. The alarm and consternation of the wives communicated itself to the husbands, and they looked solemn and concerned. The air was filled with falling water. The sound upon the myriad leaves and branches was like the roar of a cataract. We put our backs up against the great trees, only to catch a

brook on our shoulders or in the backs of our necks. Still the storm waxed. The fire was beaten down lower and lower. It surrendered one post after another, like a besieged city, and finally made only a feeble resistance from beneath a pile of charred logs and branches in the center. Our garments yielded to the encroachments of the rain in about the same manner. I believe my necktie held out the longest, and carried a few dry threads safely through. Our cunningly devised and bedecked table, which the housekeepers had so doted on and which was ready spread for breakfast, was washed as by the hose of a fire engine—only the bare poles remained—and the couch of springing boughs, that was to make Sleep jealous and o'er-fond, became a bed fit only for amphibians. Still the loosened floods came down; still the great cloud-mortars bellowed and exploded their missiles in the treetops above us. But all nervousness finally passed away, and we became dogged and resigned. Our minds became water-soaked; our thoughts were heavy and bedraggled. We were past the point of joking at one another's expense. The witticisms failed to kindle—indeed, failed to go, like the matches in our pockets. About midnight the rain slackened, and by one o'clock ceased entirely. How the rest of the night was passed beneath the dripping trees and upon the saturated ground, I have only the dimmest remembrance. All is watery and opaque; the fog settles down and obscures the scene. But I suspect I tried the "wet pack" without being a convert to hydropathy. When the morning dawned, the wives begged to be taken home, convinced that the charms of camping-out were greatly overrated. We, who had tasted this cup before, knew they had read at least a part of the legend of the wary trout without knowing it.

Locusts and Wild Honey

Droplets of water give a bubblelike texture to the surface of a fallen autumn leaf.

When one breaks camp in the morning, he turns back again and again to see what he has left. Surely, he feels, he has forgotten something; what is it? But it is only his own sad thoughts and musings he has left, the fragment of his life he has lived there. Where he hung his coat on the tree, where he slept on the boughs, where he made his coffee or broiled his trout over the coals, where he drank again and again at the little brown pool in the spring run, where he looked long and long up into the whispering branches overhead, he has left what he cannot bring away with him—the flame and the ashes of himself.

Pepacton

The Inner Vision

So often in his walks through the Catskills or Adirondacks John Burroughs would observe and marvel at wonders of nature that he had not seen before. These wonders stuck in his memory over the years, and he gradually formulated a unique impression of nature's ways. He saw nature as a renewer of itself — the dead promoting the growth of the living. Whatever happened in nature was still its way, for it fought only with itself. A spring flood would destroy, but the sun and warmth would nurture again.

He had definite ideas on how nature study should be taught, and decried those who exaggerated nature to make it more interesting. Preferring live nature to specimens in museums, Burroughs believed one could learn many scientific facts about nature from books and museums, but he could not apply these facts or learn nature's emotions until he, too, went outdoors.

Thus Burroughs walked into the forests, entered wilderness games, observed the victories and cruelties of the animal world, had the wisdom to see the beauty of weeds as well as of flowers, and quietly led others into those same pursuits and visions. Many nineteenth-century Americans left a legacy of wealth to their descendants. Some of the wealth is measurable, in thousands or millions of dollars. The wealth left by Burroughs is not measurable, but it is real.

It lies in the inner response to his writing of the twentieth-century heart. Jaded by excess, yearning for root experiences, we rejoice that one day a youth went into the wilderness, walked beside streams of clear water, lived on fresh milk and bread, and slept in an abandoned cabin.

Opposite: *Water falls in smooth cascades as it flows ceaselessly onward in Vermont. Richly colored vegetation suggests the fertility of nature.*

Nature is as regardless of a planet or a sun as of a bubble upon the river, has one no more at heart than the other. How many suns have gone out? How many planets have perished? If the earth should collide with some heavenly body today and all its life be extinguished, would it not be just like spendthrift Nature? She has infinite worlds left, and out of old she makes new. You cannot lose or destroy heat or force, nor add to them, though you seem to do so. Nature wins in every game because she bets on both sides. If her suns or systems fail, it is, after all, her laws that succeed. A burnt-out sun vindicates the constancy of her forces.

As individuals we suffer defeat, injustice, pain, sorrow, premature death; multitudes perish to fertilize the soil that is to grow the bread of other multitudes; thousands but make a bridge of their dead bodies over which other thousands are to pass safely to some land of promise. The feeble, the idiotic, the deformed, seem to suffer injustice at the hands of their maker; there is no redress, no court of appeal for them; the verdict of natural law cannot be reversed. When the current of life shrinks in its channel, there are causes for it, and if these causes ceased to operate, the universe would go to pieces; but the individual whose measure, by reason of these causes, is only half full pays the price of the sins or the shortcomings of others; his misfortune but vindicates the law upon which our lives are all strung as beads upon a thread.

In an orchard of apple trees some of the fruit is wormy, some scabbed, some dwarfed, from one cause and another; but Nature approves of the worm, and of the fungus that makes the scab, and of the aphid that makes the dwarf, just as sincerely as she approves of the perfect fruit. She holds the stakes of both sides; she wins, whoever loses. An insect stings a leaf or a stem, and instantly all the forces and fluids that were building the leaf turn to building a home for the young of the insect; the leaf is forgotten, and only the needs of the insect remembered. . . .

Leaf and Tendril

Nature does nothing merely for beauty; beauty follows as the inevitable result; and the final impression of health and finish which her works make upon the mind is owing as much to those things which are not technically called beautiful as to those which are. The former give identity to the latter. The one is to the other what substance is to form, or bone to flesh. The beauty of nature includes all that is called beautiful, as its flower; and all that is not called beautiful, as its stalk and roots.

Indeed, when I go to the woods or fields, or ascend to the hilltop, I do not seem to be gazing upon beauty at all, but to be breathing it like the air. I am not dazzled or astonished; I am in no hurry to look lest it be gone. I would not have the litter and débris removed, or the banks trimmed, or the ground painted. What I enjoy is commensurate with the earth and sky itself. It clings to the rocks and trees; it is kindred to the roughness and savagery; it rises from every tangle and chasm; it perches on the dry oak stubs with the hawks and buzzards; the crows shed it from their wings and weave it into their nests of coarse sticks; the fox barks it, the cattle low it, and every mountain path leads to its haunts. I am not a spectator of, but a participator in it. It is not an adornment; its roots strike to the center of the earth.

Birds and Poets

Emerson said that he was an endless experimenter with no past at his back. This is just what Nature is. She experiments endlessly, seeking new ways, new modes, new forms, and is ever intent upon breaking away from

the past. In this way, as Darwin showed, she attains to new species. She is blind, she gropes her way, she trusts to luck; all her successes are chance hits. Whenever I look over my right shoulder, as I sit at my desk writing these sentences, I see a long shoot of a honeysuckle that came in through a crack of my imperfectly closed window last summer. It came in looking, or rather feeling, for something to cling to. It first dropped down upon a pile of books, then reached off till it struck the windowsill of another large window; along this it crept, its regular leaves standing up like so many pairs of green ears, looking very pretty. Coming to the end of the open way there, it turned to the left and reached out into vacancy, till it struck another windowsill running at right angles to the former; along this it traveled nearly half an inch a day, till it came to the end of that road. Then it ventured out into vacant space again,

and pointed straight toward me at my desk, ten feet distant. Day by day it kept its seat upon the windowsill, and stretched out farther and farther, almost beckoning me to give it a lift or to bring it support. I could hardly resist its patient daily appeal. Late in October it had bridged about three feet of the distance that separated us, when, one day, the moment came when it could maintain itself outright in the air no longer, and it fell to the floor. "Poor thing," I said, "your faith was blind, but it was real. You knew there was a support somewhere, and you tried all ways to find it." This is Nature. She goes around the circle, she tries every direction, sure that she will find a way at some point.

Ways of Nature

When we have learned all that science can tell us about the earth, is it not more rather than less wonderful? When we know all it can tell us about the heavens above, or about the sea, or about our own bodies, or about a flower, or a bird, or a tree, or a cloud, are they less beautiful and wonderful? The mysteries of generation, of inheritance, of cell life, are rather enhanced by science.

The Breath of Life

Whose heart does not leap up, be he child or man, when he beholds a rainbow in the sky? It is the most spectacular as it is the most beautiful thing in the familiar daily nature about us. It has all the qualities that are most calculated to surprise and delight us—suddenness, brilliancy, delicacy, sharp contrasts, and the primal cosmic form, the circle. No eye so dull but turns to it with pleasure—a painted triumphal arch, yet as intangible as a dream, suddenly springing athwart the dark storm cloud. Born of the familiar and universal elements, the sun and the rain, it is yet as elusive and spectral and surprising as if it were a revelation from some other sphere. It is a kind of incarnation of the spirit of beauty—a veritable wraith that hovers and retreats before you like an angelic visitant. It is fixed there against the cloud, irrespective of the falling motion of the drops of rain through which it is formed. They fall, but it does not fall. They are swayed or whirled by the wind, but the bow keeps its place. That band of prismatic colors is in no sense a part of the rain, and the rain knows it not. It springs out in the rear of the retreating storm, but the storm knows it not. The eye knows it not, and sees it not unless placed at a certain definite point in relation to it. The point of view makes the bow. No two persons see precisely the same rainbow; there are as many bows as there are beholders.

Sometimes we see two rainbows, as if nature were in an extra happy mood. In the second one the colors are in reverse order from that of the first. The first is due to the rays of the sun falling upon the outer portions of the drops and suffering two refractions and one reflection before reaching the eye, while the second bow is due to the rays falling on the inner side of the drops and suffering two refractions and two reflections.

The rainbow is an apparition of color and form in the air. It is not so much an entity as the radiant shadow of an entity—fugitive, unreal, phantasmal, unapproachable, yet as constant as the sun and rain.

The sunset is afar off, painted upon the distant clouds, but the rainbow comes down to earth and spans the next field or valley. It hovers about the playing fountain; it beams out from the swaying spray of the cataract. It is as familiar as the day, yet as elusive as a spirit—a bow of promise, indeed—a symbol of the peace, the moderation, and the beneficence in nature that brought man upon the earth and now sustains him here.

What aeons must have passed in the history of the earth before the elements reached that harmony and equipoise which the rainbow indicates!—the sunshine following the shower, the clearing up of the weather, the obscurity and the turmoil succeeded by a cleansed and illuminated air. What aeons of warring elements before the first bit of blue sky appeared! Countless ages of mist and floods and darkness and sulphurous clouds—a rising-up of the deep and a falling-down of the heavens—before the earth saw the first smile of clear sky and the first bow of promise set in the clouds. Not till the cooling rains began to fall could life appear upon the land; not till the sun had penetrated the mists and gases that must have enveloped the earth for millions of years, could the rainbow be set on high.

"*The rainbow shall stand to me for the heaven-born
in nature and in life—the unexpected beauty and perfection
that is linked with the eternal cosmic laws.*"

It is a pleasing fancy, and it may be a scientific fact, that there were no flowering plants till the rainbow appeared. Of course the laws of optics have always been the same, but the conditions determining their operation as we see them are recent, geologically speaking. The many-colored flowering plants did not appear till long after the overburdened and superheated air had been cleared of its vapor and carbon dioxide by the rank vegetable growths that gave us our coal beds, that is, till long after Carboniferous times—probably late in Mesozoic times. With clear skies and sunshine the development of bright flower petals would take place, and with these conditions the bow would appear in the clouds. Maybe the rose and the rainbow were born on the selfsame day. At any rate, behold the bow like a flag flung out in a festive and holiday spirit, that cheers and stimulates all beholders! Festivals and holidays are exceptional in our lives, and there may be nothing strictly analogous to them in the operation of the elemental forces, but this triumphal arch so suddenly sprung across the dark abyss of the storm clouds certainly affects the beholder as a sign of gaiety and peace and good will in nature. The sunshine itself might indicate this, but the bow emphasizes it and heralds it as with banners.

The rainbow is of the earth, it is dependent upon the familiar rain, it hangs over the near field or grove, and yet it is from out the heavens; it brings the cosmic circle, the perfect curve of the sun and moon, and paints it upon the shifting mist of the storm. Not often in the organic world does nature repeat the precision of her astronomic curves and circles; in the wavelet which a dropped pebble sets going in a pool of water, in the human eye and in the eyes of some of the lower animals, and in some vegetable forms does she draw the perfect curve. Astronomy comes down to earth now

Spots covering a ladybug (left) serve to frighten its enemies. A young rabbit (opposite) busily eats a meal of tender grasses.

and then and casts its halo about familiar things.

The rainbow shall stand to me for the heaven-born in nature and in life—the unexpected beauty and perfection that is linked with the eternal cosmic laws. Nature is not all solids and fluids and gases, she is not all of this earth; she is of the heavens as well.

She is of the remote and the phenomenal; seen through man's eyes she is touched by a light that never was on sea or land. Neither is life all of the material, the tangible, the demonstrable; the witchery of the ideal, the spiritual, at times hangs the bow of promise against the darkest hours.

I do not mean to be fantastic, or to give the fact more sail than it can carry, yet I cannot but feel that the rainbow has a deep significance, and in its flitting, intangible, transmundane, yet beautiful and constant character, may well be a symbol of much that there is in nature and in life.

The Summit of the Years

Interested as I am in all branches of natural science, and great as is my debt to these things, yet I suppose my interest in nature is not strictly a scientific one. I seldom, for instance, go into a natural history museum without feeling as if I were attending a funeral. There lie the birds and animals stark and stiff, or else, what is worse, stand up in ghastly mockery of life, and the people pass along and gaze at them through the glass with the same cold and unprofitable curiosity that they gaze upon the face of their dead neighbor in his coffin. The

fish in the water, the bird in the tree, the animal in the fields or woods, what a different impression they make upon us!

To the great body of mankind, the view of nature presented through the natural sciences has a good deal of this lifeless funereal character of the specimens in the museum. It is dead dissected nature, a cabinet of curiosities carefully labeled and classified. "Every creature sundered from its natural surroundings," says Goethe, "and brought into strange company, makes an unpleasant impression on us, which disappears only by habit." Why is it that the hunter, the trapper, the traveler, the farmer, or even the schoolboy, can often tell us more of what we want to know about the bird, the flower, the animal, than the professor in all the pride of his nomenclature? Why, but that these give us a glimpse of the live creature as it stands related to other things, to the whole life of nature, and to the human heart, while the latter shows it to us as it stands related to some artificial system of human knowledge.

Indoor Studies

I am not always in sympathy with nature study as pursued in the schools, as if this kingdom could be carried by assault. Such study is too cold, too special, too mechanical; it is likely to rub the bloom off Nature. It lacks soul and emotion; it misses the accessories of the open air and its exhilarations, the sky, the clouds, the landscape, and the currents of life that pulse everywhere.

I myself have never made a dead set at studying Nature with notebook and field glass in hand. I have rather visited with her. We have walked together or sat down together, and our intimacy grows with the seasons. What I have learned about her ways I have learned easily, almost unconsciously, while fishing or camping or idling about. My desulto-ry habits have their disadvantages, no doubt, but they have their advantages also. A too strenuous pursuit defeats itself. In the fields and woods more than anywhere else all things come to those who wait, because all things are on the move, and are sure sooner or later to come your way.

Time and Change

The literary treatment of natural history themes is, of course, quite different from the scientific treatment, and should be so. The former, compared with the latter, is like free-hand drawing compared with mechanical drawing. Literature aims to give us the truth in a way to touch our emotions, and in some degree to satisfy the enjoyment we have in the living reality. The literary artist is just as much in love with the fact as is his scientific brother, only he makes a different use of the fact, and his interest in it is often of a non-scientific character. His method is synthetic rather than analytic. He deals in general, and not in technical truths—truths that he arrives at in the fields and woods, and not in the laboratory.

The essay-naturalist observes and admires; the scientific naturalist collects. One brings home a bouquet from the woods; the other, specimens for his herbarium. The former would enlist your sympathies and arouse your enthusiasm; the latter would add to your store of exact knowledge.

Ways of Nature

It is perfectly legitimate for the animal story writer to put himself inside the animal he wishes to portray, and tell how life and the world look from that point of view; but he must always be true to the facts of the case, and to the limited intelligence for which he speaks.

In the humanization of the animals, and of the facts of natural history which is supposed to be the province of literature in this field, we must recognize certain limits. Your facts are sufficiently humanized the moment they become interesting, and they become interesting the moment you relate them in any way to our lives, or make them suggestive of what we know to be true in other fields and in our own experience. Thoreau made his battle of the ants interesting because he made it illustrate all the human traits of courage, fortitude, heroism, self-sacrifice. Burns's mouse at once strikes a sympathetic chord in us without ceasing to be a mouse; we see ourselves in it. To attribute human motives and faculties to the animals is to caricature them; but to put us in such relation with them that we feel their kinship, that we see their lives embosomed in the same iron necessity as our own, that we see in

their minds a humbler manifestation of the same psychic power and intelligence that culminates and is conscious of itself in man—that, I take it, is the true humanization.

Ways of Nature

I have had a happy life, and there is not much of it I would change if I could live it over again. I think I was born under happy stars, with a keen sense of wonder, which has never left me, and which only becomes jaded a little now and then, and with no exaggerated notion of my own deserts. I have shared the common

lot, and have found it good enough for me. Unlucky is the man who is born with great expectations, and who finds nothing in life quite up to the mark.

Leaf and Tendril

I am bound to praise the simple life, because I have lived it and found it good. When I depart from it, evil results follow. I love a small house, plain clothes, simple living. Many persons know the luxury of a skin bath—a plunge in the pool or the wave unhampered by clothing. That is the simple life—direct and immediate contact with things, life with the false wrappings torn away—the fine house, the fine equipage, the expensive habits, all cut off. How free one feels, how good the elements taste, how close one gets to them, how they fit one's body and one's soul! To see the fire that warms you, or better yet, to cut the wood that feeds the fire that warms you; to see the spring where the water bubbles up that slakes your thirst, and to dip your pail into it; to see the beams that are the stay of your four walls, and the timbers that uphold the roof that shelters you; to be in direct and personal contact with the sources of your material life; to want no extras, no shields; to find the universal elements enough; to find the air and the water exhilarating; to be refreshed by a morning walk or an evening saunter; to find a quest of wild berries more satisfying than a gift of tropic fruit; to be thrilled by the stars at night; to be elated over a bird's nest, or over a wild flower in spring—these are some of the rewards of the simple life.

Leaf and Tendril

Several million years, or one million years—how can we take it in? We cannot. A hundred years is a long time in human history, and how we pause before a thousand! Then think of ten thousand, of fifty thousand, of one hundred thousand, of ten hundred thousand, or one million, or of one hundred million! What might not the slow but ceaseless creative energy do in that time, changing but a hair in each generation! If our millionaires had to earn their wealth cent by cent, and carry each cent home with them at night, it would be some years before they became millionaires. This is but a faint symbol of the slow process by which nature has piled up her riches. She has had no visions of sudden wealth. To clothe the earth with soil made from the disintegrated mountains—can we figure that time to ourselves? The Orientals try to get a hint of eternity by saying that when the Himalayas have been ground to powder by allowing a gauze veil to float against them once in a thousand years, eternity will only have just begun. Our mountains have been pulverized by a process almost as slow. In our case the gauze veil is the air, and the rains, and the snows, before which even granite crumbles. See what the god of erosion, in the shape of water, has done in the river valleys and gorges—cut a mile deep in the Colorado canyon, and yet this canyon is but of yesterday in geologic time. Only give the evolutionary god time enough and all these miracles are surely wrought.

Truly it is hard for us to realize what a part time has played in the earth's history—just time, duration—so slowly, oh, so slowly, have the great changes been brought about! The turning of mud and silt into rock in the bottom of the old seas seems to have been merely a question of time. Mud does not become rock in man's time, nor vegetable matter become coal. These processes are too slow for us. The flexing and folding of the rocky strata, miles deep, under an even pressure, is only a question of time. Allow time enough and force enough, and a layer of granite may be bent like a bow. The crystals of the rock seem to adjust themselves to the strain, and to take up new positions, just as they do, much more rapidly, in a cake of ice under pressure. Probably no human agency could flex a stratum of rock, because there is not time enough, even if there were power enough. "A low temperature acting gradually," says my geology, "during an indefinite age would produce results that could not be otherwise brought about even through greater heat." "Give us time," say the great mechanical forces, "and we will show you the immobile rocks and your rigid mountain chains as flexible as a piece of leather." "Give us time," say the dews and the rains and the snowflakes, "and we will make you a garden out of those same stubborn rocks and frowning ledges." "Give us time," says Life, starting with her protozoans in the old Cambrian seas, "and I will not stop till I have peopled the earth with myriad forms and crowned them all with man."

Time and Change

There are so many conflicting forces and interests, and the conditions of success are so complex! If the seed fall here, it will not germinate; if there, it will be drowned or washed away; if yonder, it will find too sharp competition. There are only a few places where it will

find all the conditions favorable. Hence the prodigality of Nature in seeds, scattering a thousand for one plant or tree. She is like a hunter shooting at random into every tree or bush, hoping to bring down his game, which he does if his ammunition holds out long enough; or like the British soldier in the Boer War, firing vaguely at an enemy that he does not see. But Nature's ammunition always holds out, and she hits her mark in the end. Her ammunition on our planet is the heat of the sun. When this fails, she will no longer hit the mark or try to hit it.

Ways of Nature

Don't you suppose that if the trees in the forest, the grass in the field, the fruit in the orchard, could for a moment be conscious and speak, they would each and all say, There is evil here also, there is crime, there is sin, there is struggle, defeat, and death also? One plant could complain that there is another plant stealing from it, or trespassing upon its territory and robbing it; another is being crowded to the wall, another being dwarfed by its bigger and more sturdy neighbor. . . .

Evil comes to the fruit tree in the orchard in the shape of frost that nips the fruit buds, or of worms that eat its foliage, or in the shape of birds that cut out the heart of the blossom, or in the shape of insects that lay their eggs in the baby fruit, or in the shape of fungus growths that fasten upon it and dwarf it or mar it. Evil threatens and sooner or later comes to everything that lives. Evil in this sense is a necessary part of the living universe; there is no escape from it. A world of competition, of diverse and opposed interests, is a world of struggle, of defeat, of death.

Leaf and Tendril

Perhaps there is nothing in the operations of nature to which we can properly apply the term intelligence, yet there are many things that at first sight look like it. Place a tree or plant in an unusual position and it will prove itself equal to the occasion, and behave in an unusual manner; it will show original resources; it will seem to try intelligently to master the difficulties. Up by Furlow Lake, where I was camping out, a young hemlock had become established upon the end of a large and partly decayed log that reached many feet out into the lake. The young tree was eight or nine feet high; it had sent its roots down into the log and clasped it around on the outside, and had apparently discovered that there was water instead of soil immediately beneath it, and that its sustenance must be sought elsewhere and that quickly. Accordingly it had started one large root, by far the largest of all, for the shore along the top of the log. This root, when I saw the tree, was six or seven feet long, and had bridged more than half the distance that separated the tree from the land.

Was this a kind of intelligence? If the shore had lain in the other direction, no doubt at all but the root would have started for the other side. I know a yellow pine that stands on the side of a steep hill. To make its position more secure, it has thrown out a large root at right angles with its stem directly into the bank above it, which acts as a stay or guy-rope. It was positively the best thing the tree could do. The earth has washed away so that the root where it leaves the tree is two feet above the surface of the soil.

Yet both these cases are easily explained, and without attributing any power of choice, or act of intelligent selection, to the trees. In the case of the little hemlock upon the partly submerged log, roots were probably thrown out equally in all directions; on all sides but one they reached the water and stopped growing; the water checked them; but on the land side, the root on the top of the log, not meeting with any obstacle of the kind, kept on growing, and thus pushing its way toward the shore. It was a case of survival, not of the fittest, but of that which the situation favored—the fittest with reference to position.

So with the pine tree on the side of the hill. It probably started its roots in all directions, but only the one on the upper side survived and matured. Those on the lower side finally perished, and others lower down took their places. Thus the whole life upon the globe, as we see it, is the result of this blind groping and putting forth of Nature in every direction, with failure of some of her ventures and the success of others, the circumstances, the environments, supplying the checks and supplying the stimulus, the seed falling upon the barren places just the same as upon the fertile. No discrimination on the part of Nature that we can express in the terms of our own consciousness, but ceaseless experiments in every possible direction. The only thing inexplicable is the inherent impulse to experiment, the original push, the principle of Life.

Signs and Seasons

Animal life parallels human life at many points, but it is in another plane. Something guides the lower animals, but it is not thought; something restrains them, but it is not judgment; they are provident without prudence; they are active without industry; they are skillful without practice; they are wise without knowledge; they are rational without reason; they are deceptive without guile. They cross seas without a compass, they return home without guidance, they communicate without language, their flocks act as a unit without signals or leaders. When they are joyful, they sing or they play; when they are distressed, they moan or they cry; when they are jealous, they bite or they claw, or they strike or they gore—and yet I do not suppose they experience the emotions of joy or sorrow, or anger or love, as we do, because these feelings in them do not involve reflection, memory, and what we call the higher nature, as with us.

The animals do not have to consult the almanac to know when to migrate or to go into winter quarters. At a certain time in the fall, I see the newts all making for the marshes; at a certain time in the spring, I see them all returning to the woods again. At one place where I walk, I see them on the railroad track wandering up and down between the rails, trying to get across. I often lend them a hand. They know when and in what direction to go, but not in the way I should know under the same circumstances. I should have to learn or be told; they know instinctively.

Ways of Nature

Animals are undoubtedly capable of feeling what we call worry and anxiety just as distinctly as they feel alarm or joy, only, of course, these emotions are much more complex in man. How the mother bird seems to worry as you near her nest or her young; how uneasy the cow is when separated from her calf, or the dog when he has lost his master! Do these dumb kindred of ours experience doubts and longings and suspicions and disappointments and hopes deferred just as we do?—the same in kind, if not in degree? . . .

The sheer agony or terror which an animal is capable of feeling always excites our pity.

Roosevelt tells of once coming upon a deer in snow so deep that its efforts to flee were fruitless. As he came alongside of it, of course to pass it by untouched, it fell over on its side and bleated in terror. When John Muir and his dog Stickeen, at the imminent peril of their lives, at last got over that terrible crevasse in the Alaska glacier, the dog's demonstrations of joy were very touching. He raced and bounded and cut capers and barked and felicitated himself and his master as only a dog can. . . .

A trait alike common to man and beast is imitativeness; both are naturally inclined to do what they see their fellows do. The younger children imitate the elder, the elder imitate their parents, their parents imitate their neighbors. The young writer imitates the old, the young artist copies the master. We catch the trick of speech or the accent of those we much associate with; we probably, in a measure, even catch their looks. Any fashion of dress or equipage is as catching as the measles. We are more or less copyists all our lives. Among the animals, the young do what they see their parents do; this, I am convinced, is all there is of parental instruction among them; the young unconsciously follow the example of their elders. The bird learns the song of its parent. If it never hears this song, it may develop a song of its own—like its parent's song in quality, of course, but unlike it in form. Or it may acquire the song of some other species.

Leaf and Tendril

One of our well-known natural historians thinks that there is no difference between a man's reason and a beaver's reason because, he says, when a man builds a dam, he first looks the ground over, and after due deliberation decides upon his plan, and a beaver, he avers, does the same. But the difference is obvious. Beavers, under the same conditions, build the

same kind of dams and lodges; and all beavers as a rule do the same. Instinct is uniform in its workings; it runs in a groove. Reason varies endlessly and makes endless mistakes. Men build various kinds of dams and in various kinds of places, with various kinds of material and for various kinds of uses. They exercise individual judgment, they invent new ways and seek new ends, and of course often fail.

Every man has his own measure of reason, be it more or less. It is largely personal and original with him, and frequent failure is the penalty he pays for this gift.

But the individual beaver has only the inherited intelligence of his kind, with such slight addition as his experience may have given him. He learns to avoid traps, but he does not learn to improve upon his dam or lodge building, because he does not need to; they answer his purpose. If he had new and growing wants and aspirations like man, why, then he would no longer be a beaver. He reacts to outward conditions, where man reflects and takes thought of things. His reason, if we prefer to call it such, is practically inerrant. It is blind, inasmuch as it is unconscious, but it is sure, inasmuch as it is adequate. It is a part of living nature in a sense that man's is not. If it makes a mistake, it is such a mistake as nature makes when, for instance, a hen produces an egg within an egg, or an egg without a yolk, or when more seeds germinate in the soil than can grow into plants.

A lower animal's intelligence, I say, compared with man's is blind. It does not grasp the subject perceived as ours does. When instinct perceives an object, it reacts to it, or not, just as the object is, or is not, related to its needs of one kind or another. In many ways an animal is like a child. What comes first in the child is simple perception and memory and association of memories, and these make up the main sum of an animal's intelligence. The child goes on developing till it reaches the power of reflection and of generalization—a stage of mentality that the animal never attains to.

Ways of Nature

I do not believe that animals ever commit suicide. I do not believe that they have any notions of death, or take any note of time, or even put up any "bluff game," or even deliberate together, or form plans, or forecast the seasons. They may practice deception, as when a bird feigns lameness or paralysis to decoy you away from her nest, but this of course is instinctive and not conscious deception. There is on occasion something that suggests cooperation among them, as when wolves hunt in relays, as they are said to do, or when they hunt in couples, one engaging the quarry in front, while the other assaults it from the rear; or when quail roost upon the ground in a ring, their tails to the center, their heads outward; or when cattle or horses form a circle when attacked in the open by wild beasts, the cattle with their heads outward, and the horses with their heels. Of course all this is instinctive, and not the result of deliberation. The horse always turns his tail to the storm as well, and cows and steers, if I remember rightly, turn their heads.

A family of beavers work together in building their dam, but whether or not they combine their strength upon any one object and thus achieve unitedly what they could not singly, I do not know. Of course among the bees there is cooperation and division of labor, but how much conscious intelligence enters into the matter is beyond finding out.

Leadership among the animals, when it occurs, as among savage tribes, usually falls to

the strong, to the most capable. And such leaders are self-elected: there is nothing like a democracy in the animal world. Troops of wild horses are said always to have a leader, and it is probable that bands of elk and reindeer do also. Flocks of migrating geese and swans are supposed to be led by the strongest old males; but among our flocking small birds I have never been able to discover anything like leadership. The whole flock acts as a unit, and performs its astonishing evolutions without leaders or signals.

Leaf and Tendril

I think it highly probable that the sense or faculty by which animals find their way home over long stretches of country, and which keeps them from ever being lost as man so often is, is a faculty entirely unlike anything man now possesses. The same may be said of the faculty that guides the birds back a thousand miles or more to their old breeding haunts. In caged or housed animals I fancy this faculty soon becomes blunted. President Roosevelt tells in his *Ranch Life* of a horse he owned that ran away two hundred miles across the plains, swimming rivers on the way to its old home. It is very certain, I think, that this homing feat is not accomplished by the aid of either sight or scent, for usually the returning animal seems to follow a comparatively straight line. It is, or seems to be, a consciousness of direction that is as unerring as the magnetic needle. Reason, calculation, and judgment err, but these primary instincts of the animal seem almost infallible.

Ways of Nature

So solicitous is Nature for the well-being of the offspring that she will rob the mother's body, if insufficiently nourished, to feed the baby she is carrying in her womb. If the laying hen is not properly supplied with lime material, Nature will draw it from the bones of the hen herself to build the shell of the egg The offspring is first always, and has the right of way over all else. In short, the struggle to live in the whole organic world resolves itself into the struggle to have and to rear offspring.

Under the Apple Trees

I suppose that when an animal practices deception, as when a bird feigns lameness or a broken wing to decoy you away from her nest or her young, it is quite unconscious of the act. It takes no thought about the matter. In trying to call a hen to his side, a rooster will often make believe he has food in his beak, when the pretended grain or insect may be only a pebble or a bit of stick. He picks it up and then drops it in sight of the hen, and calls her in his most persuasive manner. I do not suppose that in such cases the rooster is conscious of the fraud he is practicing. His instinct, under such circumstances, is to pick up food and call the attention of the hen to it, and when no food is present, he instinctively picks up a pebble or a stick. His main purpose is to get the hen near him, and not to feed her. When he is intent only on feeding her, he never offers her a stone instead of bread.

We have only to think of the animals as habitually in a condition analogous to, or identical with, the unthinking and involuntary character of much of our own lives. They are creatures of routine. They are wholly immersed in the unconscious, involuntary nature out of which we rise, and above which our higher lives go on.

Ways of Nature

Fear and suspicion are almost constant companions of most of the wild creatures. Even the

finches; the jays less than the starlings and the game birds. The seed-eaters and fruit-eaters are probably preyed upon much more than the purely insectivorous birds, because doubtless their flesh is sweeter.

Birds of prey have few enemies apart from man. Among the land animals we ourselves prefer the flesh of the vegetable-eaters, and the carnivora do the same. We all want to get as near to the vegetable as we can, even in our meat-eating.

Under the Apple Trees

The very idea of a bird is a symbol and a suggestion to the poet. A bird seems to be at the top of the scale, so vehement and intense is his life—large-brained, large-lunged, hot, ec-static, his frame charged with buoyancy and his heart with song. The beautiful vagabonds, endowed with every grace, masters of all climes, and knowing no bounds—how many human aspirations are realized in their free, holiday lives, and how many suggestions to the poet in their flight and song! . . .

But when the general reader thinks of the birds of the poets he very naturally calls to mind the renowned birds, the lark and nightingale, Old World melodists, embalmed in Old World poetry, but occasionally appear-ing on these shores, transported in the verse of some callow singer.

The very oldest poets, the towering antique bards, seem to make little mention of the songbirds. They loved better the soaring, swooping birds of prey, the eagle, the ominous birds, the vultures, the storks and cranes, or the clamorous seabirds and the screaming hawks. These suited better the rugged, warlike character of the times and the simple, power-ful souls of the singers themselves. Homer must have heard the twittering of the

crow, who has no natural enemies that I know of, is the very embodiment of caution and cun-ning. That peculiar wing gesture when he alights or walks about the fields—how ex-pressive it is! It is a little flash or twinkle of black plumes that tells you how alert and on his guard he is. It is a difficult problem to settle why the crow is so suspicious and cunning, since he has few or no natural enemies. No creature seems to want his flesh, tough and unsavory as it evidently is, and we can hardly attribute it to his contact with man, as we can the wildness of the hawk, because, on the whole, mankind is rather friendly to the crow. His suspicion seems ingrained, and probably involves some factor or factors in his biological history that we are ignorant of.

On the whole, it is only the birds and animals which are preyed upon that show ex-cessive caution and fear. One can well under-stand how the constant danger of being eaten does not contribute to the ease and composure of any creature, and why these which are so beset are in a state of what we call nervous-ness most of the time. Behold the small ro-dents—rats, mice, squirrels, rabbits, wood-chucks, and the like; they act as if they felt the eyes of the mink or the weasel or the cat or the hawk upon them all the time.

Among the birds some are much more ner-vous and "panicky" than others. The wood-peckers are less so than the thrushes and swallows, the cry of the plover, the voice of the turtle, and the warble of the nightingale; but they were not adequate symbols to express what he felt or to adorn his theme. Aeschylus saw in the eagle "the dog of Jove," and his verse cuts like a sword with such a conception.

It is not because the old bards were less as poets, but that they were more as men. To strong, susceptible characters, the music of nature is not confined to sweet sounds. The defiant scream of the hawk circling aloft, the wild whinney of the loon, the whooping of the crane, the booming of the bittern, the vulpine bark of the eagle, the loud trumpeting of the migratory geese sounding down out of the midnight sky; or by the seashore, the coast of New Jersey or Long Island, the wild crooning of the flocks of gulls, repeated, continued by the hour, swirling sharp and shrill, rising and falling like the wind in a storm, as they circle above the beach or dip to the dash of the waves—are much more welcome in certain moods than any and all mere bird melodies, in keeping as they are with the shaggy and un-tamed features of ocean and woods, and sug-gesting something like the Richard Wagner music in the ornithological orchestra.

Birds and Poets

Of certain game birds it is thought that at times they have the power of withholding their scent; no hint or particle of themselves goes out upon the air. I think there are persons whose spiritual pores are always sealed up, and I presume they have the best time of it. Their hearts never radiate into the void; they do not yearn and sympathize without return; they do not leave themselves by the wayside as the sheep leaves her wool upon the bram-bles and thorns.

Pepacton

A porcupine's friendly look can be deceiving. When in danger, it leaves sharp quills in the flesh of its attacker.

An Open Door to God

America one hundred years ago still had a frontier and most of the wealth of our natural resources was untapped. Our cities were rapidly growing but agriculture was the dominant activity of our citizens; the population balance had not yet turned in favor of urban dwellers. The writings of John Burroughs at this time are prophetic, for he could see the time approaching when city "rot" would begin.

Yet from the beginning to the end of his more than sixty-year writing career, Burroughs's books are illumined with his personal aspiration and his buoyant optimism regarding his fellow man. Even near the end of his life during World War I, he followed the news intensely, sure that planetary peace was finally approaching.

His preference for the countryside and its healing qualities in no way indicates any desire on his part to escape from rationality. To the contrary, Burroughs's respect for reason, together with his continual effort to achieve balance and moderation, mark his later writings. "We seem to breathe another air," he wrote, when we come to man's ethical code, surpassing anything revealed by the animal or vegetable kingdoms. The fruition of this ethical code in the lives of noble humans gave him hope for the entire race, with a deepening conviction in his later years that mankind will evolve to achieve its highest destiny.

The slightest aspect of the outdoor world reinforced his belief that an intricate plan was at work at all levels of life: The mystery of a wasp laying an egg, for example, and making special provision as if she knew in advance whether the egg would produce a male or a female, filled him with awe and assurance.

He believed that there was supreme order in the universe, that a primal source had set in motion this limitless, expanding creation, and he arrived at this, not through formalized theology or an institutionalized church, but through observing the overall perfection of the workings of nature.

Opposite: *Burroughs believed that a city dweller could be renewed and purified by the country. Even today, country is not a great distance from cities. The Palisades of New Jersey rise above the Hudson River, within sight of metropolitan New York City.*

Man has from the earliest period believed himself of divine origin, and by the divine he has meant something far removed from this earth and all its laws and processes, something quite transcending the mundane forces. He has invented or dreamed myths and legends to throw the halo of the exceptional, the far removed, the mystical, or the divine around his origin. He has spurned the clod with his foot; he has denied all kinship with bird and beast around him, and looked to the heavens above for the sources of his life. And then un-pitying science comes along and tells him that he is under the same law as the life he treads under foot, and that that law is adequate to transform the worm into the man; that he, too, has groveled in the dust, or wallowed in the slime, or fought and reveled, a reptile among reptiles; that the heavens above him, to which he turns with such awe and reverence, or such dread and foreboding, are the source of his life and hope in no other sense than they are the source of the life and hope of all other creatures. But this is the way of science; it enhances the value or significance of every-thing about us that we are wont to treat as cheap or vulgar, and it discounts the value of the things far off upon which we have laid such stress. It ties us to the earth, it calls in the messengers we send forth into the unknown; it makes the astonishing revelation—revolution-ary revelation, I may say—that the earth is em-bosomed in the infinite heavens the same as the stars that shine above us, that the creative energy is working now and here underfoot, the same as in the ages of myth and miracle; in other words, that God is really immanent in his universe, and inseparable from it; that we have been in heaven and under the celestial laws all our lives, and knew it not. Science thus kills religion, poetry, and romance only so far as it dispels our illusions and brings us back

from the imaginary to the common and the near at hand. It discounts heaven in favor of earth. It should make us more at home in the world, and more conscious of the daily beauty and wonders that surround us, and, if it does not, the trouble is probably in the ages of myth and fable that lie behind us and that have left their intoxicating influence in our blood.

We are willing to be made out of the dust of the earth when God makes us, the God we have made ourselves out of our dreams and fears and aspirations, but we are not willing to be made out of the dust of the earth when the god called Evolution makes us. An impersonal law or process we cannot revere or fear or worship or exalt; we can only study it and put it to the test. We can love or worship only per-sonality. This is why science puts such a damper upon us; it banishes personality, as we have heretofore conceived it, from the uni-verse. The thunder is no longer the voice of God, the earth is no longer his footstool. Per-sonality appears only in man; the universe is not inhuman, but unhuman. It is this discovery that we recoil from, and blame science for; and, until, in the process of time, we shall have adjusted our minds, and especially our emo-tions, to it, mankind will still recoil from it.

We love our dreams, our imaginings, as we love a prospect before our houses. We love an outlook into the ideal, the unknown in our lives. But we love also to feel the solid ground beneath our feet.

Whether life loses in charm as we lose our illusions, and whether it gains in power and satisfaction as we more and more reach solid ground in our beliefs, is a question that will be answered differently by different persons.

We have vastly more solid knowledge about the universe amid which we live than had our fathers, but are we happier, better, stronger? May it not be said that our lives consist, not in

the number of things we know any more than in the number of things we possess, but in the things we love, in the depth and sincerity of our emotions, and in the elevation of our aspirations? Has not science also enlarged the sphere of our love, and given us new grounds for wonder and admiration? It certainly has, but it as certainly has put a damper upon our awe, our reverence, our veneration. However valuable these emotions are, and whatever part they may have played in the development of character in the past, they seem doomed to play less and less part in the future. Poetry and religion, so called, seem doomed to play less and less part in the life of the race in the future. We shall still dream and aspire, but we shall not tremble and worship as in the past.

We see about us daily transformations as stupendous as that of the evolution of man from the lower animals, and we marvel not. We see the inorganic pass into the organic, we see iron and lime and potash and silex blush in the flowers, sweeten in the fruit, ripen in the grain, crimson in the blood, and we marvel not. We see the spotless pond lily rising and unfolding its snowy petals, and its trembling heart of gold, from the black slime of the pond. We contemplate our own life history as shown in our pre-natal life, and we are not disturbed. But when we stretch this process out through the geologic ages and try to see ourselves a germ, a fish, a reptile, in the womb of time, we are balked. We do not see the great mother, or the great father, or feel the lift of the great biologic laws. We are beyond our depth. It is easy to believe that the baby is born of woman, because it is a matter of daily experience, but it is not easy to believe that man is born of the animal world below him, and that that is born of inorganic Nature, because the fact is too big and tremendous.

What we call Nature works in no other way; one law is over big and little alike. What Nature does in a day typifies what she does in an eternity. It is when we reach the things done on such an enormous scale of time and power and size that we are helpless. The almost infinitely slow transformations that the theory of evolution demands balk us as do the size and distance of the fixed stars.

Time and Change

If we once seriously undertake to solve the riddle of man's origin, and go back along the line of his descent, I doubt if we can find the point, or the form, where the natural is supplanted by the supernatural as it is called, where causation ends and miracle begins. Even the first dawn of protozoic life in the primordial seas must have been natural, or it would not have occurred—must have been potential in what went before it. In this universe, so far as we know it, one thing springs from another; the sequence of cause and effect is continuous and inviolable.

We know that no man is born of full stature, with his hat and boots on; we know that he grows from an infant, and we know the infant grows from a fetus, and that the fetus grows from a bit of nucleated protoplasm in the mother's womb. Why may not the race of man grow from a like simple beginning? It seems to be the order of nature; it *is* the order of nature—first the germ, the inception, then the slow growth from the simple to the complex. It is the order of our own thoughts, our own arts, our own civilization, our own language.

In our candid moments we acknowledge the animal in ourselves and in our neighbors— especially in our neighbors—the beast, the shark, the hog, the sloth, the fox, the monkey; but to accept the notion of our animal origin,

that gives us pause. To believe that our remote ancestor, no matter how remote in time or space, was a lowly organized creature living in the primordial seas with no more brains than a shovel-nosed shark or a gar-pike, puts our scientific faith to severe test.

Time and Change

At least one thing is certain as the result of man's sojourn on this planet: he is becoming more and more at home on it, more and more on good terms with the nature around him. His childish fear and dread of it is largely gone. He now makes playfellows of things which once filled him with terror; he makes servants of forces that he once thought stood ready to devour him; he is in partnership with the sun and moon and all the hosts of heaven. He no longer peoples the air and the earth with evil spirits. The darkness of the night, or of caverns and forests, no longer conceals malignant powers or influences that are lying in wait to devour him. Even Milton speaks of

       ... this drear wood,
    The nodding horror of whose shady
      brows
    Threats the forlorn and wandering
      passenger.

To us the wood is filled with beauty and interest; the mountain is a challenge to climb to a vaster and higher outlook, and the abysmal seas hold records we would fain recover and peruse. Evil omens and prognostications have disappeared. Dread of Nature has been followed by curiosity about Nature, and curiosity has been followed by love. Men now love Nature as I fancy they have never loved her before. I fancy also that we have come to real-

A farm seems microscopic when placed among the immense White Mountains and dense forests of New Hampshire.

ize as never before the truth of the Creator's verdict upon his work: "And behold it was good."

To what do we owe this change? To the growth of the human reason led and fostered by science. Science has showed man that he is not an alien in the universe, that he is not an interloper, that he is not an exile from another sphere, or arbitrarily put here, but that he is the product of the forces that surround him.

I have no doubt that the life of man upon this planet will end, as all other forms of life will end. But the potential man will continue and does continue on other spheres. One cannot think of one part of the universe as producing man, and no other part as capable of it. The universe is all of a piece so far as its material constituents are concerned; that we know. Can there be any doubt that it is all of a piece so far as its invisible and intangible forces and capabilities are concerned? Can we believe that the earth is an alien and a stranger in the universe? that it has no near kin? that there is no tie of blood, so to speak, between it and the other planets and systems? Are the planets not all of one family, sitting around the same central source of warmth and life? And is not our system a member of a still larger family or tribe, and it of a still larger, all bound together by ties of consanguinity? Size is nothing, space is nothing. The worlds are only red corpuscles in the arteries of the infinite. If man has not yet appeared on the other planets, he will in time appear, and when he has disappeared from this globe, he will still continue elsewhere.

Time and Change

The city rapidly uses men up; families run out, man becomes sophisticated and feeble. A fresh stream of humanity is always setting from the country into the city; a stream not so fresh flows back again into the country, a stream for the most part of jaded and pale humanity. It is arterial blood when it flows in, and venous blood when it comes back.

A nation always begins to rot first in its great cities, is indeed perhaps always rotting there, and is saved only by the antiseptic virtues and fresh supplies of country blood.

Signs and Seasons

Science has banished the arbitrary, the miraculous, the exceptional, from nature, and instead of these things has revealed order, system, and the irrefragable logic of cause and effect. Instead of good and bad spirits contending with one another, it reveals an inevitable beneficence and a steady upward progress. It shows that the universe is made of one stuff, and that no atom can go amiss or lose its way.

Leaf and Tendril

179

Man takes root at his feet, and at best he is no more than a potted plant in his house or carriage till he has established communication with the soil by the loving and magnetic touch of his soles to it. Then the tie of association is born; then spring those invisible fibres and rootlets through which character comes to smack of the soil, and which make a man kindred to the spot of earth he inhabits.

Winter Sunshine

Man has no wings, and yet he can soar above the clouds; he is not swift of foot, and yet he can outspeed the fleetest hound or horse; he has but feeble weapons in his organization, and yet he can slay or master all the great beasts; his eye is not so sharp as that of the eagle or the vulture, and yet he can see into the farthest depths of siderial space; he has only very feeble occult powers of communication with his fellows, and yet he can talk around the world and send his voice across mountains and deserts; his hands are weak things beside a lion's paw or an elephant's trunk, and yet he can move mountains and stay rivers and set bounds to the wildest seas. His dog can out-smell him and out-run him and out-bite him, and yet his dog looks up to him as to a god. He has erring reason in place of unerring instinct, and yet he has changed the face of the planet.

Without the specialization of the lower animals—their wonderful adaptation to particular ends—their tools, their weapons, their strength, their speed, man yet makes them all his servants. His brain is more than a match for all the special advantages nature has given them. The one gift of reason makes him supreme in the world.

Time and Change

To say that the world or the order of nature is reasonable is like saying how well the body fits the skin. The order of nature fits our faculties and appears reasonable to us, not because it is shaped to them, but because they are shaped to it, just as the eye is shaped to the light or the ear to the waves of sound. Nature is first and man last.

The Light of Day

O to share the great, sunny, joyous life of the earth! to be as happy as the birds are! as contented as the cattle on the hills! as the leaves of the trees that dance and rustle in the wind! as the waters that murmur and sparkle to the sea! To be able to see that the sin and sorrow and suffering of the world are a necessary part of the natural course of things, a phase of the law of growth and development that runs through the universe, bitter in its personal application, but illuminating when we look upon life as a whole! Without death and decay, how could life go on? Without what we call sin (which is another name for imperfection) and the struggle consequent upon it, how could our development proceed? I know the waste, the delay, the suffering in the history of the race are appalling, but they only repeat the waste, the delay, the conflict through which the earth itself has gone and is still going, and which finally issues in peace and tranquillity. Look at the grass, the flowers, the sweet serenity and repose of the fields—at what a price it has all been bought, of what a warring of the elements, of what overturnings, and pulverizings and shiftings of land and sea, and slow grindings of the mills of the gods of the fore-world it is all the outcome!

Leaf and Tendril

It is well to stop our star-gazing occasionally and consider the ground under our feet. Maybe it is celestial, too; maybe this brown, sun-tanned, sin-stained earth is a sister to the morning and the evening star. If it should turn out to be so, it seems to me we have many things to learn over again—we must tear down and build larger.

No wonder the old fathers resisted the notion that the earth was round and turned round! It was not the millponds that were in danger of spilling out so much as certain creeds and theories. Once set the earth afloat and what have you not unloosed? Admit that the notch in the mountain really does not determine where the sun shall rise—or,

further, that this great palpable fact, which our senses so overwhelmingly affirm, of the passage of the sun from east to west over the earth, is no fact at all, but an illusion—that it is the solid ground beneath our feet that is slipping away, and not the sun up there—and you have admitted a principle that makes your creeds and philosophies whirl like soap bubbles. Your creeds and philosophies are based on a different fact, proceed from different premises, and are totally inadequate to face such a deduction.

It is a source of wonder to me how modern theology has stood for so long a time the test of astronomy—in fact, has harnessed astronomy into its service. It is not that the stars are less convincing, but that men are harder to convince than I was willing to believe. It is not difficult to see how this fantastic conception of things would fall before the standard of him who had got even the instincts or the minutest fact of nature. How, then, can it prevail before him whose standard is the globe—"round, rolling, compact"—with no possible failures, of no conceivable age, obeying no namable rule or method, yet above all rule and method— purely an inspiration, whose vast beauty and perfection the highest speech can only edge?

Our proudest statements go but a little way—at most but recognize this as up, that as down, that as east, this as west, but absolutely, without reference to point or place which way is east and which way west? Leave the earth behind you as a speck in the sky, and which way is up, which down? Now where is your immutable fact? Enlarge your sphere of observation a little, take into account the circle, instead of the fragment of an arc, and how relative and puerile your boasted achievements seem! It is as if sight were added after groping with the hands.

Are the great facts of science, then, only so many formulae—have they no moral applica-tion? Does it make no difference in your views of God, of the soul and immortality, whether the earth is all or whether there are other earths, whether it is round or flat, whether it moves or remains at rest? Do you reason and speculate the same under Kepler's laws as under Ptolemy's spheres?

What a tremendous assurance is that simple assertion of the astronomer that the earth is a star! How it satisfies one, infinitely more than all preaching, theories, or speculations whatever! What does it not settle? I will not doubt or fear any longer. This day I have a new faith. Let the preacher preach, let the theorists contend, let the old incessant warfare go on—the sky covers all, and the elements administer to all the same, and, undisturbed, the "divine ship sails the divine sea."

The Light of Day

The more we know matter, the more we know mind; the more we know nature, the more we know God; the more familiar we are

with the earth forces, the more intimate will be our acquaintance with the celestial forces.

The Breath of Life

The scientific faith of mankind—faith in the universality of natural causation—is greatly on the increase; it is waxing in proportion as theological faith is waning: and if love of truth is to be our form of love of God, and if the conservation of human life and the amelioration of its conditions are to be our form of brotherly love, then the religion of a scientific age certainly has some redeeming features.

Under the Apple Trees

What appears more real than the sky? We think of it and speak of it as if it was as positive and tangible a fact as the earth. See how it is painted by the sunset or by the sunrise. How blue it is by day, how gemmed by stars at night. At one time tender and wooing, at another hard and distant. Yet what an illusion! There is no sky; it is only vacancy, only empty space. It is a glimpse of the infinite. When we try to grasp or measure or define the Power we call God, we find it to be another sky, sheltering, over-arching, all-embracing—palpable to the casual eye, but receding, vanishing to the closer search....

The Light of Day

The Infinite cannot be measured. The plan of Nature is so immense—but she has no plan, no scheme, but to go on and on forever. What is size, what is time, distance, etc., to the Infinite? Nothing. The Infinite knows no time, no space, no great, no small, no beginning, no end.

I sometimes think that the earth and the worlds are a kind of nervous ganglia in an organization of which we can form no conception, or less even than that. If one of the globules of blood that circulate in our veins were magnified enough million times, we might see a globe teeming with life and power. Such is this earth of ours, coursing in the veins of the Infinite. Size is only relative, and the imagination finds no end to the series either way.

Birds and Poets

There surely comes a time when the mind perceives that this world is the work of God also and not of devils, and that in the order of nature we may behold the ways of the Eternal; in fact, that God is here and now in the humblest and most familiar fact, as sleepless and active as ever he was in old Judea. This perception has come and is coming to more minds today than ever before—this perception of the modernness of God, of the modernness of inspiration, of the modernness of religion; that there was never any more revelation than there is now, never any more miracles or signs and wonders, never any more conversing of God with man, never any more Garden of

Eden, or fall of Adam, or thunder of Sinai, or ministering angels, than there is now; in fact, that these things are not historical events, but inward experiences and perceptions perpetually renewed or typified in the growth of the race. This is the modern gospel; this is the one vital and formative religious thought of modern times.

The mind that has fully opened to this perception no longer divorces its faith from its reason, no longer rests in the idea of a dualism in creation or opposition between God and the world, and cannot feel at ease until its religious belief is in harmony with its natural knowledge. The two must not be at war. What we hope for, what we aspire to, must be consistent with what we know. Faith and science must, indeed, go hand in hand. The conception of religion as a miraculous scheme for man's redemption interpolated into history, God's original design with reference to man having miscarried, is entirely undermined and overthrown by the perception of the unity and consistency of creation as revealed by science.

The Light of Day

The old school Baptists look upon themselves as the elect, the chosen few, the remnant that is to be saved, and they treat all other claimants to an interest in the Celestial City as pretenders. It was to bring them forth that the whole creation groaned and travailed in pain all the ages. How they snort at divinity schools, Sunday schools, missionaries, protracted meetings, paid and educated clergymen, prepared sermons, etc. Only he who is called of God can preach (how true!), and he shall take no thought of what he is to say until he gets into the pulpit. Hence the sermons I frequently listened to in my youth, that were supposed to be the direct inspiration of the Creator of heaven and earth, were of a kind to make Blair turn gray in an hour. But how can the carnal mind understand these things!

I am bound to say that the God of our neighbor was a more benevolent and merciful God than the one my father believed in. He wanted all to be saved, whether they would be or not, while the other had carefully provided that only a part could or should be saved.

The disputants of course never succeeded in changing each other's views, but only in causing them to be held more tenaciously. They both as old men died in the faith they had early professed. It was sufficient unto them while they lived, and at the last it did not fail them. Father always spoke of his approaching end with perfect assurance and composure. He looked upon it as some journey he was about to make, some change of scene that was to come to him, and which need give him none but happy anticipation. I remember that once while visiting him, a few years before his death, he told me he was reading the Bible through again. He had just been reading the story of Elijah and the false prophets. He told me the story, and when he came to where the fire came down from heaven and consumed Elijah's offering, his emotion overcame him, and he broke down completely. He no more doubted these things, he no more doubted the literal truth of every passage in the Bible, than he did his own existence.

How impossible for me to read the Bible as father or Jerry did, or to feel any interest in the questions which were so vital to them; not because I have hardened my heart against these things, but mainly because I was born forty years later than they were, with different tastes and habits of mind. The time spirit has wrought many changes in men's views, and I have seen the world with other eyes and through other mediums.

The Light of Day

184

Portrait of a Naturalist

John Burroughs's sojourn in this world was filled with the problems which centuries do not seem to change. During his eighty-four years, he experienced rejection as a child; real financial hardship as a student; loneliness as a young schoolteacher in Illinois, far from his Catskill birthplace; war (in this case, the Civil War, seen sometimes from near the front lines when the battles moved close to his Washington, D.C., home); middle years of travel, writing and increasing honor from the world; gradually meeting the sorrow through the deaths of many of his friends and relatives, with quiet, closing years. Even these were marred by the convulsions of World War I and the death of his wife, Ursula.

In the same way that the problems of his life were the eternal problems confronting each person in this world, his life's work had an eternal theme. Burroughs saw the planet as a divine ship, furnished by the Creator with adequate supplies for all its inhabitants for the full length of its journey. He experienced awe, looking at the slightest portion of these provisions. A weed, a bird in the air, a chipmunk at his window, a blade of grass or a beehive could evoke his meditation on the eternal. He was concerned, ahead of most of his countrymen, that this ship be kept in good repair, that the delicate balance of nature not be disturbed by thoughtless action or greed on the part of one generation. He regarded the wilderness areas and the countryside of America as a fountain, pouring fresh abundance into urban areas and refreshing city dwellers threatened with the loss of their human inheritance.

In more than twenty books and numerous articles written over a sixty-five-year period, Burroughs proved to be far ahead of his time in grasping the need for a rational approach to conservation in America. He rarely wrote directly on this subject; nevertheless, at the end of any of his books the reader is left with a feeling of concern that nature's riches be protected. Without lectures, without moralizing, Burroughs takes you into his experiences with plant and animal life. He invites you to come with him to the Catskills, to the Adirondacks, to Hawaii, to Alaska with equally famous naturalist John Muir, to Yellowstone with President Theodore Roosevelt, to Yosemite and Grand Canyon. As if it were natural to be in his presence, you make these journeys with him as your wise, compassionate guide.

He does not speak from lofty heights, or humble you with his confident knowledge. In simple language, of one friend to another, he tells you of the wonders he saw on his walks last spring or summer. The winter months were usually his time for writing, drawing on the wealth of what nature revealed to him the previous seasons. In later life, when he went more into philosophical subjects, his language still retained the quaint expressions of his youth. Complex subjects are handled in a way that language aids our comprehension, rather than becoming one more barrier between us and the issue.

Opposite: *"In the more open spaces the woods mirror themselves in the glassy surface till one seems floating between two worlds...."*

John Burroughs

Perhaps the tales spun by his grandfather, a soldier-farmer who had seen service under General George Washington in the Revolutionary War, helped to keep Burroughs close to central issues and simple ways. These tales were filled with spooks and goblins, source of a fear which affected Burroughs's early experiences with nature, but in his early teens that fear vanished as the beauty of the wilderness tracts around his home became known to him.

As the seventh of ten children, born in 1837 to a family which had little regard for book learning, Burroughs surmounted many obstacles to achieve literary distinction and a number of honorary degrees from universities such as Yale. He developed such loving insight and knowledge about nature, beginning with the Catskill area in which he grew up, that this became the storehouse of his creativity. His modest books, reporting what he had seen with refreshing

(continued on page 191)

John Burroughs (above) at the age of 25, the year in which he wrote his first poem, "Waiting." In later years (opposite), Burroughs meditated about the deeper meanings of nature.

189

*Burroughs's house, Riverby, at West
Park, N.Y. (opposite), is a charming structure.
At nearby Black Creek Falls (above), he enjoyed
the "wild of a little different flavor."*

enthusiasm, brought him small though sufficient monetary rewards to support
him as a full-time writer and brought, also, respectful attention from his
readers, who included such contemporary greats as Thomas Edison, Walt
Whitman and Henry Ford.

He used to comment in later life that he was happy to have been protected
from the dangers of too much financial return from his writing. This, he
thought, would have been a test, but the small rewards he received were the
source of happiness and quiet comfort for his family. Burroughs's father could
read, write and do simple arithmetic; his mother could only read. From this
background, Burroughs found his way into the literary world and was the
source of his parents' support during the closing years of their lives.

From the age of seventeen, Burroughs wrote down his thoughts and events
in a journal, together with sporadic efforts to write articles. His first one was
published anonymously, but conjecture about the author led him to reveal his
identity and from that time he was a productive and frequently published
author.

Burroughs's chestnut-bark study at Riverby (below)
provided a natural setting for him to work. One of his favorite
pastimes (right) was fishing in a quiet stream.

The many humiliations he suffered as a child, so different from the rest of his family, left deep scars. He recalled a number of times the moment of shame when his father proudly urged him, in front of a watchful hotel landlord, to drive a wagon load of butter through a narrow barn door, only to have the wagon get stuck. He also remembered the time he was urged to invite a fourteen-year-old girl to walk home from an apple-paring party. His intense shyness made this an impossibility, for he couldn't manage the necessary words. In later life, he spoke before distinguished audiences and traveled in the West as the personal guest of President Theodore Roosevelt, but the memory of his early shyness helped him retain a gentle manner and an awareness of the feelings of others.

That same sensitivity, turned outward into the world of nature, gathered treasures for his readers. In the preface to *The Summit of the Years*, published in 1913 when he was seventy-six years old, he writes:

There is no other joy in life like mental and bodily activity, like keeping up a live interest in the world of thought and things. Old age is practically held at bay so long as one can keep the currents of his life moving. The vital currents, like mountain streams, tend to rejuvenate themselves as they flow.

One reaps his harvest, and it looks as if his acres would never yield another, but lo! as the seasons return, there springs a fresh crop of ideas and observations. It seems as if one never could get to the end of all the delightful things there are to know, and to observe, and to speculate about in the world. Nature is always young, and there is no greater felicity than to share in her youth.

194

Burroughs loved observing the wilderness on gentle walks through the woods (opposite). In his rustic cabin, Slabsides (above), he could observe nature from a secluded vantage point.

I still find each day too short for all the thoughts I want to think, all the walks I want to take, all the books I want to read, and all the friends I want to see.

Burroughs lived in a time of vast changes in American society. The American landscape, at the end of his life, already showed the beginnings of technological invasion. His legacy to his reader is a careful, human accounting of days spent in natural areas and in outdoor pursuits. Things contrary to fact do not creep into his writing, for he found sufficient beauty in what is true to leave no place for the untrue.

The fruit of a man's life is often apparent at the end of it. Lives spent negligently may leave a bitter taste, but lives spent in service yield qualities of spirit which enrich all who come close. In any of John Burroughs's books, you taste the honesty, reverence for life, and quiet appreciation of the gifts of this planet which filled his adult years. He lived a full life and today we enjoy the fruit of it.

In the preceding pages, excerpts from twenty of his books offer glimpses of the acute observation and deep tenderness of this American naturalist. His eye saw, his heart responded, and from this union his pen set down word pictures to inspire and delight coming generations.

— Beth McKenty

Rough logs (opposite and above) reveal the fundamental structure of Burroughs's retreat at Slabsides. By living at such a basic level, he could better reflect about the mysteries of the wilderness.

Right: *John Burroughs (far left)
is seated at camp with friends, among them
Harvey Firestone (second from left), Henry Ford
(fourth from left) and Thomas Edison (fifth from
left). Opposite, bottom: Burroughs and President
Theodore Roosevelt enjoy a campfire in Yellowstone National Park. Below: A letter from Roosevelt to Burroughs reveals the affection and
respect these two men had for each other.*

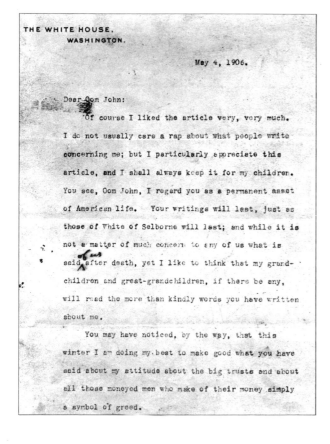

THE WHITE HOUSE,
WASHINGTON.

May 4, 1906.

Dear Oom John:

Of course I liked the article very, very much.
I do not usually care a rap about what people write
concerning me; but I particularly appreciate this
article, and I shall always keep it for my children.
You see, Oom John, I regard you as a permanent asset
of American life. Your writings will last, just as
those of White of Selborne will last; and while it is
not a matter of much concern to any of us what is
said after death, yet I like to think that my grand-
children and great-grandchildren, if there be any,
will read the more than kindly words you have written
about me.

You may have noticed, by the way, that this
winter I am doing my best to make good what you have
said about my attitude about the big trusts and about
all those moneyed men who make of their money simply
a symbol of greed.

I have just come in from walking around the
White House grounds with Mrs. Roosevelt and wishing
heartily you were with us to tell us what the various
warblers were. Unfortunately, I haven't a natural
history book with me at the moment. Most of the
warblers were up in the tops of the trees and I could
not get good glimpses of them; but there was one with
chestnut cheeks, with bright yellow behind the cheeks
and a yellow breast thickly streaked with black, which
has puzzled me. Doubtless it is a very common kind
which has for the moment slipped my memory. I saw
the blackburnian, and the summer yellowbird, and the
black-throated green.

Affectionately yours,

Theodore Roosevelt

John Burroughs, Esq.,

198

John Burroughs and John Muir (opposite, top) were at home in the wilderness. Burroughs relaxes in a chair at Woodchuck Lodge (right), his summer home near Roxbury, N.Y. Seated in his nearby haybarn study (below), he devotes some time to his writing. Woodchuck Lodge (opposite, bottom) is located on his boyhood farm, which held many memories for him.

Burroughs was fond of teaching children (below) the beauty of nature. He also enjoyed outdoor cooking (opposite), especially in the company of friends such as Farida Wiley, who has devoted her life to the John Burroughs Memorial Association.

Chronology

(Books are listed under publication dates)

1837—Burroughs born on farm near Roxbury, New York, April 3, to Chauncey A. and Amy Kelly Burroughs

1844-54—Attended rural schools

1854-63—Taught school, mostly in New York, one winter (1856-57) in Buffalo Grove, Illinois, and one winter (1858-59) in Newark, New Jersey; attended two colleges for short periods

1856—First appearance in print: article on philosophy, anonymously credited

1857—Married Ursula North from Tongore, New York

1859-60—Wrote various philosophical essays for leading magazines

1861—Wrote first nature essays, "From the Back Country," for New York publication

1862—Wrote first poem, "Waiting"

1863—Began to study birds; resigned as teacher and moved to Washington, D.C.; met Walt Whitman

1864—Appointed clerk in Treasury Department

1867—First book published: *Notes on Walt Whitman as Poet and Person*

1871—First European visit; *Wake-Robin*

1872-74—Resigned as clerk, moved back to Catskills, appointed as Federal bank examiner; built Riverby at West Park, New York

1875—*Winter Sunshine*

1876—Began keeping regular journal

1877—*Birds and Poets*

1878—Birth of his son, Julian

1879—*Locusts and Wild Honey*

1881—Built chestnut-bark study at Riverby; *Pepacton*

1882—Second European visit

1884—*Fresh Fields*

1885—Resigned bank examining position

1886—*Signs and Seasons*

1889—*Indoor Studies*

1894—*Riverby*

1895—Began building Slabsides in woods near Riverby

1896—*Whitman: A Study*

1899—Joined Harriman Alaskan Expedition; met John Muir

1900—*The Light of Day*

1901—*Squirrels and Other Fur Bearers*; edited *Songs of Nature* (poems)

1902—Traveled to Jamaica; *Literary Values*; *Life of Audubon*

1903—Traveled to Yellowstone with President Roosevelt

1904—*Far and Near*

1905—*Ways of Nature*

1906—*Bird and Bough* (poems)

1907—*Camping and Tramping with Roosevelt*

1908—Established summer home (Woodchuck Lodge) on farm of his boyhood; *Leaf and Tendril*

1909—Traveled with John Muir in Far West; visited Hawaii

1910—Received Doctor of Letters degree from Yale University

1911—Second trip to California; received Doctor of Humane Letters degree from Colgate University

1912—*Time and Change*

1913—*The Summit of the Years*

1915—Received Doctor of Letters degree from University of Georgia; *The Breath of Life*

1916—*Under the Apple Trees*

1917—Death of his wife, Ursula

1919—Third trip to California; *Field and Study*

1920—Fourth trip to California; *Accepting the Universe*

1921—Died March 29 while returning from California; *Under the Maples*; John Burroughs Memorial Association founded

1922—*The Last Harvest*

1925—*The Life and Letters of John Burroughs* edited by Clara Barrus

1926—First Burroughs Medal awarded

1928—*The Heart of Burroughs' Journals* edited by Clara Barrus

*Burroughs spent many hours at work in Slabsides. This 1920
photograph is believed to be the last one ever taken of him.*

Remembering John Burroughs

When I was very small I thought of John Burroughs as the man who brought grapes and peaches when he came to visit us, the man who walked with us in meadows and lanes and woodsy places, the man whose white hair and beard turned pink under the study lamp where he sat in the evenings and talked about books and people and the outdoors, and, best of all, the man who had a sort of magic about him. . . .

And when we went to visit him in his cabin in the woods which he called Slabsides, I remember it smelled like the outdoors, for there was bark on the furniture and walls. At night there was a funny bird outside that said "Whip-poor-will!" over and over. The little house that smelled like the woods, and the strange talking bird, were part of the wonderful world John Burroughs knew about and showed to us. . . .

Later, at Woodchuck Lodge, his summer home in the Catskills, I saw that here—even more than in the other places where I had known him—Mr. Burroughs seemed to delight in his surroundings. He faced his bed on the porch toward the east. "Those first bright rays of the sun," he would say. "How can anyone want to miss them?"

And with the same relish he welcomed the less spectacular events of the day—the smell and taste of his breakfast bacon, his chores in the garden and woodshed, his writing in the open door of the haybarn, his walks over the hill or up to the Boyhood Rock in the pasture. It was a relish that spread to everyone around him. . . .

I recall once seeing him pick grapes. So gently he would lay the clusters in the basket it was like a mother putting her baby in the cradle. "To keep the bloom on them," he explained. Watching him, it seemed at the moment that I would never love anything as I loved those dusty blue grapes. And apples! He would cup one in his hand, pull it gently from the branch, feel of it, smell it, before placing it lovingly in the barrel. Later, in the winter, as

Burroughs's gravesite is appropriately situated on the farm of his boyhood in his beloved Catskills.

he fondled an apple, raised it to his nose, I knew he was seeing again the hills and the blue sky that backgrounded the day when he had picked it. And I, too, would see them. . . .

Most contagious of all was his enjoyment of the days. During my summers at Woodchuck Lodge I had discovered the joy of walking in the fields and woods. I remember meeting him once on an especially bright day during his last fall there. His eyes sparkled as he spoke of the day. "Can't you think of some way we can take hold of its coattails and not let it get away?"

For me, and I'm sure for most of the people who knew him, and for the readers of his books as well, he has done just that—grabbed the days, the outdoors, all natural things and sprinkled on them a magic that has made them memorable and kept them from ever really getting away from us.

—Harriet Barrus Shatraw

207

Appendix

Winners of the Burroughs Medal

The Burroughs Medal is awarded periodically by the John Burroughs
Memorial Association, Inc., to distinguished authors for books in the field of nature
writing. Since 1926, over forty authors have received this prestigious award.

1926 – William Beebe; *Pheasants of the World*

1927 – Ernest Thompson Seton; *Lives of Game Animals*

1928 – John Russell McCarthy; *Nature Poems*

1929 – Frank M. Chapman; *Handbook of North American Birds*

1930 – Archibald Rutledge; *Peace in the Heart*

1932 – Frederick S. Dellenbaugh; *A Canyon Voyage*

1933 – Oliver Perry Medsgar; (set) *Spring; Summer; Fall; Winter*

1934 – W. W. Christman; *Wild Pasture Pine*

1936 – Charles Crawford Ghorst; *Recordings of Bird Calls*

1938 – Robert Cushman Murphy; *Oceanic Birds of South America*

1939 – T. Gilbert Pearson; *Adventures in Bird Protection*

1940 – Arthur Cleveland Bent; *Life Histories of North American Birds*

1941 – Louis J. Halle, Jr.; *Birds Against Man*

1942 – Edward Armstrong; *Birds of the Grey Wind*

1943 – Edwin Way Teale; *Near Horizons*

1945 – Rutherford Platt; *This Green World*

1946 – Mr. & Mrs. Francis Lee Jaques; *Snowshoe Country*

1948 – Theodora Stanwell-Fletcher; *Driftwood Valley*

1949 – Mr. & Mrs. Allan D. Cruickshank; *Flight Into Sunshine*

1950 – Roger Tory Peterson; *Birds Over America*

1952 – Rachel Carson; *The Sea Around Us*

1953 – Gilbert Klingel; *The Bay*

1954 – Joseph Wood Krutch; *The Desert Year*

1955 – Wallace B. Grange; *Those of the Forest*

1956 – Guy Murchie; *Song of the Sky*

1957 – Archie Carr; *The Windward Road*

1958 – Robert Porter Allen; *On the Trail of Vanishing Birds*

1960 – John Kieran; *Natural History of New York City*

1961 – Loren C. Eiseley; *The Firmament of Time*

1962 – George Miksch Sutton; *Iceland Summer*

1963 – Adolph Murie; *A Naturalist in Alaska*

1964 – John Hay; *The Great Beach*

1965 – Paul Brooks; *Roadless Area*

1966 – Louis Darling; *The Gull's Way*

1967 – Charleton Ogburn, Jr.; *The Winter Beach*

1968 – Hal Borland; *Hill Country Harvest*

1969 – Louis deKiriline Lawrence; *The Lovely and the Wild*

1970 – Victor B. Scheffer; *The Year of the Whale*

1971 – John K. Terees; *From Laurel Hill to Siler's Bog*

1972 – Robert Arbib; *The Lord's Woods*

1973 – Elizabeth Barlow; *The Forests and Wetlands of New York City*

1974 – Sigurd F. Olson; *Wilderness Days*